# POPE JOHN
## A LIFE O...

© Wyatt North Publishing, LLC 2018

Publishing by Wyatt North Publishing, LLC. A Boutique Publishing Company.

"Wyatt North" and "A Boutique Publishing Company" are trademarks of Wyatt North Publishing, LLC.

Copyright © Wyatt North Publishing, LLC. All rights reserved, including the right to reproduce this book or portions thereof in any form whatsoever. For more information please visit http://www.WyattNorth.com.

Cover design by Wyatt North Publishing, LLC. Copyright © Wyatt North Publishing, LLC. All rights reserved.

Scripture texts in this work are taken from the *New American Bible, revised edition*© 2010, 1991, 1986, 1970 Confraternity of Christian Doctrine, Washington, D.C. and are used by permission of the copyright owner. All Rights Reserved. No part of the New American Bible may be reproduced in any form without permission in writing

Thanks for reading, have one on me.

Readers like you keep me motived to write, and I appreciate your support.

Please consider visiting my site at www.wyattnorth.com where you can learn more and signup for complimentary books.

Thanks again for reading.

- Wyatt

**Chapter One: Introduction** ............................................................ 6

Disciple ........................................................................................... 8

Communicator ............................................................................. 11

About This Biography ................................................................. 13

**Chapter Two: The First Act** ..................................................... 15

Birth ............................................................................................. 16

School .......................................................................................... 20

Theater ........................................................................................ 23

University .................................................................................... 27

**Chapter Three: Under the Third Reich** ................................. 30

Invasion ....................................................................................... 31

Opposition ................................................................................... 35

Birth of a Mystic ......................................................................... 41

Theater of Resistance ................................................................. 44

Underground Seminary .............................................................. 47

The Communist Occupation ...................................................... 53

**Chapter Four: Wojtyla the Priest** ............................................ 56

Ordination ................................................................................... 57

Doctoral Dissertation ................................................................. 60

A Polish Priest ............................................................................. 64

Bishop Wojtyla and Vatican II ................................................... 70

**Chapter Five: Archbiship of Krakow** ...... 74

Vatican II ...... 75

Poland's Bishop ...... 81

Cardinal Wojtyla ...... 85

Humanae Vitae ...... 90

**Chapter Six: The Election of John Paul II** ...... 94

The September Papacy ...... 95

Setting the Stage ...... 98

**Chapter Seven: The Pope as Pastor and Evangelist** ...... 102

A Pope from Galilee ...... 103

Changing the World ...... 106

Going Home ...... 110

A Second Act? ...... 113

Theology of the Body ...... 115

Other Writings and Acts ...... 120

Aging Gracefully ...... 125

**Chapter Eight: Sainted and Remembered** ...... 128

# Chapter One: Introduction

If he and his avant-garde theater troupe were caught performing their "theater of the living word," they could have been sentenced to a death camp. Still, the twenty-two-year-old Karol Józef Wojtyla paid no attention to illegitimate demands of Poland's Nazi occupiers. The poem he recited, Adam Mickewicz's *Pan Tadeusz,* on November 28, 1942, would have particularly irritated the Nazi authorities. The poem, which celebrates the resilience of the Polish spirit, features a revolt of the Poles against their former Russian occupiers. The message was clear: the Polish spirit could overcome Nazi oppression. As an actor, and a student at an underground seminary, the young Wojtyla defied the Nazis fearlessly on multiple fronts.

Thirty years later, Wojtyla, now Pope John Paul II, stood to address his native country again. Having survived the Nazi occupation, the Poles now faced another obstacle to Polish liberty. This time, the pope addressed not a small crowd in a darkened room, but the largest assembly ever to gather on Polish soil, and his target on this occasion was communism. Unlike with the Nazis, whom the Poles universally regarded as enemies, he was likely to encounter more people who sympathized with the communists' ideals. Still, at the conclusion of his speech, the crowd was convinced. "We want God!" was the chant that spontaneously followed the pope's address.

On neither occasion did Wojtyla speak from purely political motivations. His concern was not economic, nor did it have to do with the power and influence Poland might have within the world. Instead, he spoke from a disciple's heart. He championed the cause of the Polish people not in order to inspire a spirit of nationalism, but in order to give them hope and to safeguard the dignity that was already theirs on account of the life, death, and resurrection of Jesus Christ.

# Disciple

Pope St. John Paul II was known for many things. In his youth, he had a passion for the theater. He eventually became one of the most charismatic and influential bishops in the Roman Catholic College of Cardinals. That a Pole should be elevated to the papacy shocked many within the church and around the world. During his long pontificate, he was one of the most beloved, but also most controversial, people in the world. Still, in order to understand what motivated his life, it is crucial to understand that he was—above all else—a thoroughly devoted and convicted disciple of Jesus Christ.

Several biographers have noted that John Paul II viewed himself ultimately as a disciple of Jesus Christ. This conviction gave him the courage to oppose Nazism and communism. While several popes before him had viewed their task largely as the CEO of the Roman Catholic Church, and engaged primarily in notable and respectable managerial tasks, Pope John Paul II believed that the chair of St. Peter was preeminently an evangelist's seat.

Pope John Paul II appeared on the world's stage during the second half of the twentieth Century. It was a time when many people, following several brutal wars around the world, had given up on the ideals put forth in the Enlightenment of three centuries prior. Former utopian optimism for a better world, prizing human liberty and dignity above all else, had given way to a spirit of cynicism. Such worldwide pessimism had also been ascribed to the Church. The decline of Christendom in Europe, especially, was a symptom of a world that had lost all hope for a better tomorrow.

In order to chart a course into the future, however, Pope John Paul II proclaimed a hopeful message rooted in the words of someone who had spoken nearly two thousand years earlier. The God who had assumed His place amongst us in the person of Jesus Christ was not, in his view, an irrelevant voice from a naïve past. The message of Jesus Christ was one that survived everything—even when the human spirit had waned in the wake of the world wars and the rise and failures of communism.

# Communicator

John Paul II was the most visible pope in history. He was also among the Church's greatest communicators ever. Some of this he owed to his experience as an actor and a powerful orator. He also owed something to the era during which he served as pope. He was the first to fully leverage the power of the media to communicate his hopeful message around the world. As he traveled to more countries than any pope before him, visiting nearly every corner of the world, television made him relatable even to those within and outside the church who never had the chance to meet him personally. He set a precedent that the two popes who have followed, Pope Benedict XVI and Pope Francis, have emulated.

John Paul II just missed the advent of social media. Had it been available, in his time, he undoubtedly would have leveraged its power as the Church's prime evangelist. Still, the opportunities John Paul II pursued during his tenure upon the chair of St. Peter necessarily set the tone for how the Church continues to engage the world on an even wider scale today.

# About This Biography

This is not a typical biography. For those primarily interested in the facts of Pope John Paul II's life, start to finish, there are several biographies better suited to providing those details. In fact, this biography is not chiefly about John Paul II's life at all. Instead, this is a biography about the meaning and message to which John Paul II dedicated his life. This is a biography of faith, hope, and love. And for Pope St. John Paul II, as for St. Paul, the greatest of these was love.

Accordingly, there may be details about the pope's life that would be essential in a traditional biography but might not be featured in this volume. Other details that might be minimized in other biographies, in turn, might receive special attention here.

Arguably, Pope John Paul II was one of the most misunderstood figures in the twentieth century. *Time* magazine declared him their Man of the Year in 1994. He had played a pivotal role in ending the Cold War, so for some, Pope John Paul II was a champion of freedom and peace. Others, who had a more liberal vision for the Church than he espoused, decried the pope as a dogmatic authoritarian, out of touch with the direction in which the world was heading. Even as many Catholics thanked the Lord for his leadership and influence, others prayed for his demise.

Beloved by most, especially in memory, he was one of the most influential *and* controversial figures of his time. Such is not at all atypical of a saint. In fact, Jesus had told His disciples not to be surprised when people oppose them, persecute them, or speak evil of them on His account (Luke 6:22). In spite of his critics, Pope John Paul II remained a bold, courageous, and devoted servant of the Church. He was a disciple, evangelist, and a real-world embodiment of Jesus' command to "love one another, as I have loved you" (John 15:12).

# Chapter Two: The First Act

# Birth

Karol Józef Wojtyla was born May 18, 1920, only months before First Marshall Józef Klemens Piłsudski dealt a decisive blow against the invading Russian Soviets at the Battle of Warsaw. This victory assured that Poland's newfound independence, first secured in 1918, would endure. This meant, in effect, that Wojtyla was amongst the first generation of Poles who would grow up in freedom in more than 150 years. He grew up under the Second Polish Republic, at a time when liberty was considered fragile and could not be taken for granted.

While the political winds blowing through Poland were undoubtedly formative in Wojtyla's life, these facts alone cannot account for the man he ultimately became. If such were the case, nearly every Pole in the early twentieth century would have changed the world. Still, raised in an environment where liberty was cherished, and tyranny was not merely a threat in the nation's memory but also remained a present possibility, he was conditioned to understand the importance of human liberty for the flourishing of the human spirit.

As a child, Wojtyla was nicknamed "Lolek," likely to distinguish the junior Wojtyla from his father, Karol Wojtyla. It was also an appropriate name, reflecting the Polish spirit of the times—"Lolek" means "free man." The elder Karol served as a lieutenant in the Polish army until he retired in 1927. His mother, Emilia, mastered embroidery and sold her work to contribute to the family's modest income.

Sadly, while Lolek was only in the third grade, on April 13, 1929, his mother Emilia died of kidney failure and congenital heart disease at the age of forty-five. Catholic scholars have long hypothesized how the death of his mother at a young age might have impacted young Karol. Some suggest that his deep-seated Marian piety emerged to fill the void of maternal affection that was lacking in his childhood. Speaking autobiographically, however, John Paul II later mentioned that he had no "clear awareness" of his mother's contribution to his spiritual life and religious training. In truth, it seems, Karol had few memories of his mother.

Most remarkably, it has been observed how incredible it is that the man who, arguably, offered Christendom the greatest and profoundest twentieth-century contribution to understanding the biblical view of marriage—by way of his book *Love and Responsibility*, in addition to his famed *Man and Woman He Created Them: A Theology of the Body*—did so with no personal experience in marriage and with very little experience observing his parents' marriage as a child.

The young Lolek, however, was deeply influenced by his father in religious matters. Later in life, the pope reflected on how his father was a "man of constant prayer," who could be found on his knees each morning making supplication to the Lord. The young Karol prayed the rosary and read the Bible with his father frequently. According to biographer George Weigel, "Lolek also learned from his father that manliness and prayerfulness were not antinomies." Fatherhood, in fact, was an "icon" of God communicating the nature of God's desired relationship with the world. This is not to say that one should define God's role as Father by viewing Him in light of our earthly fathers, who often fall short of their responsibilities. Rather, fathers should look to God to understand what being a good father truly means. Wojtyla viewed fatherhood as a vocation of love that compelled one toward generosity—"giving birth," as it were, through selfless acts and charitable giving.

While his father taught him to honor and respect the visible institution of the church, he also encouraged his son to consider the church as a mystery, with an invisible dimension that transcends the structures and institutions of Rome. Even as Christ Himself is greater than His sacraments, it is in those gifts that one can be sure He is found in mercy and grace. Since the

Church is the body of Christ by virtue of being the Lord's bride, one-in-flesh, the Church herself shares in this mystery. This means that while one can never say for certain what God's judgment might be for those outside of the Church, one can never dismiss them. By virtue of their human dignity, originally created in the image of God, all human beings should be honored and respected, their liberty guarded and protected against tyranny and godlessness. John Paul II once wrote, concerning his father, that while they never spoke about a call to the priesthood, "his example was in a way my first seminary, a kind of domestic seminary."

By his own admission, in his childhood the young Karol was particularly impacted by Jesus' address to His disciples in Luke 12:32: "Fear not, little flock, it is your Father's good pleasure to give you the kingdom." The admonition not to fear meant that there was much, apart from God's good pleasure, His disciples might fear. There would be persecutions. There would be hard-hearted persons who would reject their proclamation concerning the Kingdom of God. They might suffer at the hands of the godless. Accordingly, while the gospel offers a promise, it is not an *easy* promise. God does not "zap" away suffering and discomfort in His disciples' lives. Instead, God promises endurance. He promises, on account of His "good pleasure" to give them His kingdom, that the trials and tribulations of this world will be temporary. There is a better, eternal future upon which men and women can fix their eyes in confidence to see them through the difficulties of this life. The path to the crown goes through the cross.

# School

In addition to the "domestic seminary" he experienced under his father's tutelage, the young Karol met Father Kazimierz Figlewicz in 1930 when the latter came to Marcin Wadowita State Secondary School to teach the catechism and to prepare parish altar boys for assisting the priests during Mass. It was likely Father Figlewicz who first planted the seed that becoming a priest might be a possibility in Karol's future. He became Karol's father confessor, and even after Father Figlewicz was transferred to Krakow, he invited Karol—now in high school—to join him for the Holy Week services at the cathedral. This trip made a "profound impression" upon the eventual pope as he himself later reflected.

During his school years, Karol grew very close to his older brother, Edmund, who was studying to become a physician. Shortly after Edmund graduated and assumed a position at a hospital in Bielsko, he contracted scarlet fever from one of his patients and died on December 5, 1932. He was only twenty-six years old, and Karol was twelve at the time. The event apparently had a profound impact on Karol, possibly even more so than the death of his mother. The inscription on Edmund's tombstone reflected Karol's own understanding of his brother's death: it described Edmond as "a victim of his profession, sacrificing his young life in the service of humanity."

For the young Karol, though his brother's death was tragic, it also taught him a profound respect for the mystery of God's will. Serving God inevitably meant self-sacrifice, and often for the most faithful of His disciples, this sacrifice resulted in the termination of one's earthly life. Why God takes some early, and permits other faithful disciples to live into old age, is a mystery that one should not bother to ask. In the grand scheme of God's kingdom, in comparison to eternity, the longevity of a human life is relatively insignificant. What matters, rather, is the fidelity with which one follows the example of Christ, particularly in terms of self-sacrifice. In this respect, a shortened life of a godly man is greater eternally than the long life of a wicked or godless person.

When the archbishop of Krakow, Adam Stefan Sapieha, paid a visit to Karol's secondary school in 1938, he was impressed with the young Karol. He asked the chaplain whether it might be possible to make Wojtyla into a priest. However, due to Karol's plans to attend Jagiellonian University to study theater and literacy, the priest told the archbishop it was unlikely. Apparently the archbishop declared it "a pity."

# Theater

It is not altogether a surprise, despite the young Wojtyla's piety and devotion, that he would first set his passions upon literature and the theater. He was not the only young Pole who took to literature and drama at the time. Often, a priest who did not initially pursue religious studies brings a unique and invaluable perspective to the priesthood. Such was undoubtedly the case with Karol Wojtyla.

Polish Romanticism emerged in a climate when the revolutionary literature of the nineteenth century was in vogue. Yet, the Poles examined the revolutionary spirit of the day from a perspective unique when compared to the rest of Europe. While many Europeans viewed revolution as a way of breaking from the past, and leaving behind ancient institutions (including Christianity), the romantic perspective of the Poles believed that revolution implied precisely the opposite. The past is not to be overthrown or "moved beyond," but renewed. A Polish revolutionary, therefore, was not likely an agnostic and certainly was not an atheist. For a Pole to be a revolutionary meant a profound commitment to Christian doctrine and morality, springing from the streams of Catholicism.

Accordingly, Wojtyla was conditioned by the spirit of Polish Romanticism to see a solution for the plight of modernity that most secular thinkers in the twentieth century thought long defunct and antiquated. He believed that the Christian faith was not a relic of the past, but an objective truth that envelops all of human history, from the beginning until the Parousia and the coming of the Kingdom of God.

In 1936 the sixteen-year-old Wojtyla was taken under the wing of Mieczyslaw Kotlarczyk. While the relationship between the Church and the theater historically had often been tense, if not downright adversarial, during the Polish Romantic period, many saw the two institutions as two different voices by which God could speak to the world. Kotlarczyk explicitly adopted this view, indicating in his own writings than an actor is a sort of priest who illuminates God's transcendent truth through a "theater of the inner word." Through a well-constructed theatrical performance, the universal truths of Christendom could speak to the heart of God's people in ways that traditional preaching struggled to do. The key was to ensure that the performers prized the message, the "word," above external impressions and the spectacle of a show.

Through the heavy influence of Polish Romanticism and the tutelage of Kotlarczyk, the seeds of some of the future pope's most profound influences had already been planted. For example, based on his participation in the theater, Wojtyla learned how the emotions and intellect engage in a human psyche to reveal truth. Rather than viewing the emotions as an enemy of the intellect, or vice versa, Wojtyla learned that the human being was created by God with both emotional and intellectual capacities. One's perception of truth and experience of God's Word doesn't depend solely on either an emotional response to a powerful testimony or an intellectual mastery of dogmatic truth. A Christian encounters God as a total person, emotionally and intellectually all at once. This truth unlocks the secret of how God uses His word to transform history and culture. It also explains the approach that Wojtyla took later, as a pope who was undoubtedly a giant amongst intellectuals but also a compassionate and charismatic visionary, capable of inspiriting people on an emotional level.

The theater also taught Wojtyla the importance of community. In a performance, the actors, director, stage hands, and other crew constituted a highly disciplined combination of diverse individuals, with a variety of talents, who blended their abilities together to create something that none of them could produce individually. In the end, the community of the theater worked to create something greater than the sum of its parts.

It also led to more esoteric reflection regarding the nature and destiny of man and God's plan and purpose for the world. If the dramatic could connect people to universal truths, for example, might there be something about universal truth, human life, and all of reality that is innately dramatic? There is a reason, for instance, why the biblical gospel is frequently termed the "greatest story ever told." Modernity's division between drama and truth, between a story and hi*story,* fails to consider why the most popular works of fiction engage themes from history—one of the most common being the death/resurrection motif, exemplified by a protagonist's selfless sacrifice. Is it perhaps the case that we perceive our real lives in terms of stories because we find reality more interesting when we fictionalize it? Or, rather, is it that we are attracted to certain stories precisely because they connect us to universal or historical truths that are larger than ourselves? Clearly, the lessons that Wojtyla learned at a young age as a budding young actor cohered with the latter rather than the former.

# University

Wojtyla pursued his interests further when he decided to attend Jagiellonian University in the fall of 1938. The university was founded in 1364, and from the time of the Reformation and Counter-Reformation through the Enlightenment, the university stood at the intersection of classical Christianity and humanism. Copernicus, for instance, whose heliocentric cosmology challenged traditional church teaching, had studied at the Jagiellonian. In this respect, Wojtyla's collegiate education prepared him for the role he would later serve as pope, bridging the gap between modernity and Christendom while recognizing that the latter was not rendered obsolete by the former, but is actually invigorated by it.

While at the Jagiellonian, Wajtoyla took a keen interest in linguistics. He indicated in a letter that language was a mystery and that "without language there would be no literature." Language, he came to recognize, played a pivotal role in how humans understand the world, how they engage one another, and how they relate to God. Of course, his passion for the theater remained. Following the 1937–1938 academic year, for instance, a performance he gave gained the attention of Poland's most famous actor at the time, Juliusz Osterwa, who saw the play and invited Wojtyla and his cast to his apartment after the show. He and Wojtyla stayed in contact afterward, undoubtedly fueling the fire of Wojtyla's passion for the theater.

Also during this era, Wojtyla became a vocal opponent of the rising tide of antisemitism that was spreading throughout Europe, including Poland. He joined the Circle of Scholars of Polish Studies, a group of students interested in curriculum reform, and opposed the restrictions placed on Jews who wished to study at the Jagiellonian. Yet, this "free son" of Poland saw, in his college years, a proud nation abandoned by its allies and forced to negotiate with Moscow and Berlin. Neither of these totalitarian regimes could tolerate the sort of liberty that had defined Poland during Wojtyla's childhood and adolescence.

Accordingly, with his many gifts and devout piety, Wojtyla became increasingly aware that a time was coming when he might be forced to choose between remaining faithful to God and bending the knee to earthly brutes. He was raised to value liberty as an essential component of human happiness as well as to be keenly aware of how fragile liberty is. It is something that must be fought for, in some way, by every generation. Therefore, it was no surprise to him that his nation's liberty was once again threatened. Moreover, he knew from a young age that he could never relinquish liberty under the threat of any brute or totalitarian force.

# Chapter Three: Under the Third Reich

# Invasion

Germany invaded Poland on September 1, 1939, beginning the Second World War. Only two months later, 184 of Wojtyla's professors at the Jagiellonian University were arrested and deported, forcing the young academic and actor to further his studies in secret, even as he participated in activities intended to resist the German occupiers. Roughly 18 percent of the 35 million Poles who resided there were either killed in combat or murdered by the Gestapo during the course of World War II.

Wojtyla's experience during the war was undoubtedly formative and likely played a pivotal role in his decision to enter the priesthood. From September 1939 through January 1945, the Polish people were under a struggle for both literal and moral survival. Faithful martyrs, whose names the Poles remember but most of the world has forgotten, rose to the occasion and purchased a powerful testimony at the cost of their lives. For example, Maximillian Kolbe, a Franciscan priest, sacrificed his own life for the sake of a fellow prisoner when the prisoners were ordered to be starved to death at Auschwitz. Indeed, the six years spent under Nazi occupation were times defined by both unimaginable cruelty and acts of valiant heroism.

As a result, how World War II shaped people's worldviews—not only in Poland, but throughout the world—depended upon one's focus. For some, the horrors of the war and the dreadful inhumanity exhibited in the holocaust resulted for some in a perspective that everything was meaningless, that progress was a vain pursuit, and that life was absurd. For those like Karol Wojtyla, the horrors of the time only confirmed what the Church had always believed regarding the perversion of sin in the world and testified to the power of a human spirit infused by faith. The cross of the war gave way to resurrection, a victory that taught the world, not just the Poles, that freedom was precious and fragile.

After Poland was conquered in 1939, different portions of the previously unified country were occupied by different foreign powers. The eastern part of Poland was effectively absorbed by the Soviet Union. The central and western regions of Poland were ruled by the Germans, with certain parts of Poland incorporated into the Third Reich.

A declaration of Hans Frank, who governed from Poland's Wawel Castle, sent instructions to his subordinates dictating the way they should treat the Polish people: "The Pole," Frank wrote, "has no rights whatsoever. His only obligation is to obey what we help him... Every vestige of Polish culture is to be eliminated... There will never again be a Poland." The war waged against the Poles was not merely a matter of seizing their lands and resources. It was about stamping out a culture that the invaders deemed inferior. Accordingly, to participate in any distinctly Polish celebration of cultural activity was considered a capital offense. Any crime of resistance would be punished either by immediate execution or by transferral to a concentration camp—which usually was only a delayed version of the same punishment.

Since the Catholic Church was at the heart of Polish culture, it also became a target for Nazi repression. Still, in contrast to some other nations, where the clergy were often complicit with the Nazi agenda, many Polish priests and laymen alike stood against their oppressors. During the war, 3,646 Polish priests were imprisoned, and 2,647 were executed. The Nazis arrested 1,117 nuns, executing 238 while 25 more died from other causes associated with their captivity. At least 120 priests were subjected to inhumane medical experiments at the hands of the Nazis.

Of course, these horrors were spread out across the six-year period when Poland was occupied, and it was not until after the war ended that the Poles could survey their losses and react with appropriate shock at the collective trauma they had experienced. At first, in fact, the biggest sacrifice Wojtyla was forced to make was effectively giving up his acting career. In a letter he wrote to Kotlarczyk in November 1939, he mentioned that the Germans had seized a playhouse, where he had hoped to find a part-time job, for their own use. As fate would have it, however, Wojtyla had not seen his last stage.

# Opposition

The once proud Jagiellonian University reformed itself as an underground school by the start of 1942. Wojtyla was one of 800 students who enthusiastically continued his education in the re-formed school, even as most lectures took place at night in private homes. The 136 professors who boldly taught in the underground school risked their very lives for their defiance.

If the young Wojtyla had learned to prize liberty due to a keen awareness of how fragile it is, the same can be said regarding his attitude toward education. The great risk his professors had to assume in order to teach him and his classmates left a profound impression upon him regarding the value of education—136 instructors believed it was worth more than, potentially, their lives—and he came to understand that opportunities to learn can never be taken for granted.

Accordingly, John Paul II's intellectualism flowed not from a mere interest in academic topics but from a keen awareness that learning is a great privilege and that the more one knows regarding the truth of things, the closer one is to the mind of God. Still, while the modern man who lives in relative peace might believe that education is purely an academic or mental pursuit, for Wojtyla, learning was also a manner of worshiping God. To show a keen interest in the truth that God has written into the world and inspired through human beings is to honor God Himself. Consequently, the division between mind and heart was not so neat and clean in Wojtyla's experience. It is always the whole person, including mind and heart and perhaps more, who is called to take up his cross and follow Christ. It is the whole person who becomes a disciple when called by the gospel through the Holy Spirit. It is the whole person who receives a sacrament—for instance, one is not only baptized in the body, but the whole person is thereby buried with Christ and raised anew.

These lessons, and others, were impressed upon Wojtyla as his faith was tried by the oppressive Nazis. Of course, he could not devote all his energies to learning. Under the General Government, every able-bodied male at least fourteen years old and younger than sixty was required to work. Without an *Arbeitskarte*, or work card, he could not stay in Krakow. For a while, Wojtyla worked for a restaurant as a store messenger. Since it was not particularly vigorous or tiring work, it enabled him to pursue his academic interests when off the clock. After 1940, however, Wojtyla was forced to change jobs, and for nearly four years, he was forced to engage in intense manual labor for the Solvay chemical company. He often worked in a quarry in intense temperatures (during the winter of 1940–41 temperatures dipped to -22 degrees Fahrenheit/-30 degrees Celsius). He spent his days shoveling limestone, and they were only allowed a single fifteen-minute break daily. Those Poles who could not cut it, depending upon the work they were assigned, risked deportation to Germany.

Under the strain of hard labor, however, Wojtyla was not distracted from living the disciple's life. He often engaged in debates with one of his atheist coworkers, who had been a member of the Polish Socialist Party. Some of his coworkers from the time later reported that they often saw him on his knees in prayer in the midst of their labors in spite of the mockery of some of the other workers. When Pope John Paul II reflected on this period of his life, he indicated that the strain of the situation drove him to seek Christ more fervently, rather than distract him from his faith, as it did for some.

Moreover, he recalled that while working in the chemical factories, he read the works of St. Louis Grignon du Montfort, a French preacher who lived in the eighteenth century. His study revealed that the Marian piety he had practiced in his youth was somewhat misguided. When one shows proper devotion to Mary, he found, it is always so that one might draw closer to Christ Himself by imitating the Mother of God. Genuine Marian piety should drive one into a closer and more intense relationship with Christ—for Mary herself could be said to have been the Lord's very first disciple. This, in turn, leads to a closer relationship with the Holy Trinity and a participation in the mysteries of Incarnation and Redemption.

His time engaged in hard labor also led to new meditations on the meaning of work. Work is not merely a job that one performs in order to get by. While Adam and Eve were cursed to work in pain, it is not the work itself that is the curse, but the pain that accompanies it. For Wojtyla, work in spite of pain becomes a participation in God's own work, His creativity, and puts the human being in touch with the original purpose for which God first placed man in the Garden: to exercise God's very dominion over the earth. This dominion, of course, was not the sort of dominion that Wojtyla experienced under the cruel hand of the German occupiers. This dominion was a sort of rule that proceeded from God's own character—a rule that served every subject, every creature whom God Himself prized. The dominion that one exercises must always be dominion in God's image and likeness. This means ruling from the posture of a servant who willfully creates and provides and who gives of himself freely, without expectation for something in return.

These insights, first nurtured under the grueling pace of hard labor, proved formative for John Paul II in how he would later discuss love in general. It forms his basis for understanding the relationship between man and woman in his famous lectures on the Theology of the Body. It forms the foundation for his premise in *Love and Responsibility*, that love is linked to action as one takes ownership of one's responsibility for another person. In 1956, fifteen years after the fact, Wojtyla took pen to paper and crafted a poem reflecting on his experience as a hard laborer under Nazi rule:

> *Listen, when cadences of knocking hammers so much their own*

> *I transfer into our inner life, to test the strength of each blow—*
>
> *Listen: electric current cuts through a river of rock—*
>
> *Then the thought grows in me day after day,*
>
> *The whole greatness of this work dwells inside a man.*

His reflections indicate a conviction that doing work is something that sets human beings apart as creatures made in God's image. Animals do not work. They may be busy, and they may instinctively go about doing what needs to be done to survive, but an animal does not work—not in the same way that human beings do. Human beings work for more than survival; they work because of love. A father labors to provide for his family and children. A mother might work the same way in today's world, but even if she remains at home, she works out of love to nurture her children and ensure the wellbeing of the family.

Still, since Adam and Eve fell into sin, work involves pain and toil. The earth does not readily yield to man's efforts. There is a sort of wrestling involved in labor, which puts mankind into touch with a kind of "fundamental anger" or frustration that is often tied to the forces that frustrate one's work. This anger, however, is an inevitability on account of the fact that human labor is properly understood as an act of love. When one works from a position of love, one cannot help but grow angry when one's loving efforts are thwarted or undermined—particularly by other human beings, but also by the natural tension man experiences during labor with the earth that does not readily consent with man's will and instead responds only to the sweat of his brow. The tension between love and anger, both inherent in human work, is resolved only when one upholds a transcendent understanding of human dignity. With this understanding, anger does not overcome the loving impetus that spurs us to work. Instead, it becomes a righteous anger, rightly acknowledging that the creation itself groans for the fulfillment of redemption promised in Christ.

Indeed, redemption is a theme that emerges in Wojtyla's youthful reflections. God habitually relies on painful, and even sinful, experiences to draw human beings into closer communion with Him. That the labor imposed upon Wojtyla due to the German occupation should lead him to deeper reflections upon the nature of work and love, according to God's design in the beginning, seems to some an absurd conclusion. Many people invoke their struggles and toils as an excuse to discount God's goodness, and they thereby further separate themselves from God by blaming Him for their suffering. Wojtyla, however, recognized in the image of the cross, above all else, that God regularly arrests the purposes of evil men in order to manifest His kingdom in the world. This does not mean that evil is somehow less troublesome. It does not render God the "author" of evil. It does not mean, either, that one's suffering on account of evil is lessened. It does mean, however, that faith sees—even in the midst of evil and suffering—a God who is at work to work all things for good for those who love Him. God is so much greater than evil, and His purposes and plans so beyond human understanding, that the deeds of evil men become means by which God works His will in the lives of His people.

# Birth of a Mystic

It was also during the period of Nazi occupation that Wojtyla first discovered mysticism. Sometime during 1940, at a gathering of young people at his local parish, Karol Wojtyla met Jan Tyranowski. Tyranowski had no formal religious training. He had no formal position in the Church hierarchy. Yet, he had spent a large portion of his life devoting himself to Catholic spirituality and possessed a sizable library of spiritual classics. As he met with the young men at the parish, who were vigorously discussing a number of points of doctrine, he insisted that the issues they were exploring were no abstractions. For Tyranowski, what the young men debated as "doctrines" were not topics to master, but the objects of his daily piety and experience.

Tyranowski's position in the parish became more prominent after a May 1941 raid by the Gestapo. Several parishes were closed, and a number of priests were arrested. The remaining parish priest at St. Stanislaw Kostka asked Tyranowski to take the young men who remained at the parish under his wing, to continue the parish's youth ministry on his own since the parish lacked a priest to do so. The group grew rapidly, and Tyranowski soon was forced to appoint leaders from the group who could conduct what he called the "Living Rosary." Wojtyla was among the first of the leaders Tyranowski chose, and subsequently tutored in spiritual disciplines. Later, Wojtyla reflected that Tyranowski had taught him and the rest of the youth that religion actually shapes souls and that religious truths were not merely "interdictions" or "limitations" but the avenue by which one comes to participate in the "life of God." According to Wojtyla, the way that Tyranowski lived his life proved "that one could not only inquire about God but that one could live with God."

Amongst Tyranowski's most lasting impacts on Wojtyla was his introduction of Wojtyla to the writings of St. John of the Cross, whose Carmelite mysticism embraced a spirituality consisting of abandonment. This form of mysticism advocates that God is truly met when one "abandons" pursuing Him through one's intellect, emotions, or senses. It is in the "dark night" when God seems most absent that one comes closest to the state of mind experienced by Jesus when He was forsaken upon the Cross. Thus, one must completely surrender to God in order to experience His presence. Since surrender and self-sacrifice are expressions of love, it is ultimately love that defines the Carmelite approach to abandonment. It means letting go of the worldly ways of pursuing security and, instead, opening oneself to God, who meets us in the void and delivers us, through the cross, to the resurrection.

It is worth noting how starkly this approach contrasted with the Nazi "will to power" that undergirded Hitler's fascist ideology. Imitating Christ, and effectively claiming no power of one's own even if it belongs to oneself by matter of right (see Philippians 2), is precisely the opposite of the Nazi path to power, which prized strength of will above all else.

As a leader of a Living Rosary group, Wojtyla was effectively responsible for fifteen other young lives, who together pursued their spiritual path in defiance of the Nazis. His spiritual discipline, as a result, was bolstered by an awareness that more than his own spiritual wellbeing was at stake. By taking responsibility for others, in fact, he learned more deeply what it means to love and, in turn, this responsibility ushered him into a closer relationship with God. The influence of Tyranowski and the disciplines he practiced as a Living Rosary leader also changed the way Wojtyla experienced prayer. While Wojtyla had always been devout, undoubtedly imitating the example his father had provided him, prayer had always been a matter of intercession or contemplation. From Tyranowski, however, he learned that through prayer he could effectively enter God's presence and that the experience of prayer could vivify every aspect of his life.

# Theater of Resistance

As Wojtyla matured in a spiritual sense, he continued to pursue his interest in the theater, even though the Germans had engaged in a thorough campaign to eradicate Polish culture, of which the theater was a significant part. He and his friends found that the persecution of actors and other stakeholders in the theater did not dissuade them at all but, rather, seemed to invigorate them with a sense of a greater purpose. They saw themselves as the protectors of the Polish heritage, and it would fall to them, at some point in the future, to see it resurrected.

Beginning in 1939, Wojtyla penned some plays of his own. His first, which has now been lost, was entitled *David*, supposedly a dramatic piece rooted in biblical stories as well as Polish history. When he wrote *Job* in the spring of 1940, he interpreted the biblical story in such a way as to draw parallels between Job's circumstances and Poland's place under Nazi oppression. In the same year, he wrote *Jeremiah*, which re-framed the biblical story in the era of the sixteenth-century Counter-Reformation and featured a Jesuit preacher named Piotr Skagra, who was fighting for the Polish nation's soul and dignity. Clearly, this historical episode was meant to inspire the Poles who were searching for answers—i.e., why Poland was now suffering under the heel of evildoers.

Often, Wojtyla and his actor friends would prepare and stage performances, typically in someone's apartment with audiences of thirty or fewer persons. This form of underground theater did not come with the same kind of notoriety that Karol was accustomed to seeing actors enjoy. One such actor, Juliusz Osterwa, had been forbidden by the Nazis to perform. He and Wojtyla collaborated to translate classical works, and Osterwa attended at least one of Karol's underground performances. It seems, however, that the older actor was too accustomed to fame as it had existed before the war to find satisfaction in underground performances. Wojtyla and his friends believed they were doing something important—for them, this was not a job or a way of achieving notoriety, but a mission. Osterwa simply lacked the future pope's passion, and his celebrity was detracting from the deeper purposes for which the secret theater troupe was formed.

When the Germans invaded the Soviet Union, Mieczyslaw Kotlarczyk moved to Krakow, and eventually he and his wife found a home with Wojtyla. Kotlarczyk's notion of a "theater of the word" was meant to be a form of protest against the Nazis' attempt to exterminate Polish culture. After an organizational meeting held on August 22, 1941, under Kotlarczyk's leadership and with Wojtyla's support and participation, the troupe—later known as the Rhapsodic Theater—was born. Aside from Kotlarczyk, all of the actors and volunteers were in their late teens or twenties. Twice-a-week rehearsals were conducted at different times of the day, and in various venues, in order to avoid casting suspicion upon their gatherings. If they had been caught, they would likely have become victims of a Nazi firing squad. Accordingly, the group was very selective about the admission of new members and even about whom they invited to attend their performances.

During the course of the war, the Rhapsodic Theater managed to produce seven unique productions, totaling twenty-two performances. With hundreds of rehearsals, it is remarkable that the clandestine theater survived undetected. Their purpose was not merely to entertain Polish people—though this would have been a worthy endeavor in its own right due to the destitution many had experienced, and the people undoubtedly would have appreciated the escape that a theatrical performance offered. Rather, their goal was to save the Polish culture from Nazi extermination. Their mission was motivated by the New Testament truth that God's people are called to speak truth to power, even if doing so means sacrificing their lives.

# Underground Seminary

Karol Wojtyla's father died in 1941, leaving him the last survivor of his family before he had turned twenty-one. To lose so much at such a young age can have a profound impact on a man. This impact was compounded by the fact that during the Nazi occupation, he was surrounded by death: the death of Jewish persons he knew and respected, the arrest and sometimes the execution of his own professors as well as many priests, and the casualties of the war. In the wake of such frequent and brutal death, Wojtyla often found himself alone, in a cruciform position on his floor, in prayer.

By his own recollection, Karol Wojtyla began to consider his career plans in 1941 and the beginning of 1942. The sheer amount of death and destruction he witnessed gave him a profound sense of what he called a "progressive detachment" from his earlier plans. In the wake of his father's recent death, moreover, he reflected further on the "domestic seminary" in which he had been raised by following his father's pious example. Increasingly, he even interpreted his time in the theater as a sign that he was being prepared for the priesthood.

In the fall of 1942, Karol Wojtyla approached the residences of the archbishops of Krakow and Franciszkanska and asked to be considered as a candidate for the priesthood. He was accepted into the seminary shortly thereafter.

It didn't take long after the Nazi invasion before the Gestapo began demanding that the seminary be stripped of any credentialed professors and reduced to a sort of trade school that might offer pragmatic instruction (i.e., how to conduct the Mass) but no theological education. With the archbishop's support, however, the seminary ignored these demands and continued to conduct classes as usual. In response, the Gestapo banned the enrollment of new seminary students. Again, the archbishop defied the Nazi demand and instead hired would-be seminarians as parish secretaries, then invited them to clandestine courses held on the seminary premises. They did not wholly evade the Gestapo, however. On one occasion, a raid resulted in the arrest and execution of five seminarians. In response, the archbishop determined to re-establish the seminary completely underground. A seminary student was sworn to secrecy—he could tell no one he was studying for the priesthood. Classes were often held in homes or parishes, and only rarely would the same place be used to host a class more than one time consecutively.

The underground seminary began small, only allowing ten students the opportunity to study. Karol Wotjyla was among this first group of ten. Even while studying in secret, he maintained his similarly forbidden practice of performing with the Rhapsodic Theater. The fact that Wotjyla was not caught engaging in either activity, some have observed, was nothing short of miraculous. Spending so much time devoted to forbidden tasks, he would have had difficulty accounting for his daily activities if he were ever interviewed by the Gestapo.

Though enrolled as a clandestine seminarian undoubtedly posed its own challenges, what Pope John Paul II later remembered as his biggest challenge at the time was his exposure to philosophy. Given that Wotjyla had long been steeped in the Polish Romantic literary tradition, turning to texts on metaphysics, Aristotle, and Thomas Aquinas posed a new kind of challenge. The language was dense, rarely appealed to common human emotions, and seemed, on the surface, far removed from the concerns of daily life. Still, he persisted. As he later recognized, it took a couple of months of "hacking" his way through the "vegetation" before he came to a clearing and discovered "the deep reasons for what until then I had only lived and felt ... [and] what intuition and sensibility had until then taught me about the world found solid confirmation."

This was a pivotal point in the development of Pope John Paul II as a theologian. While many tend toward either emotional literature or, alternatively, academic works, and struggle embracing the other, he developed a well-rounded appreciation of literature of any sort that reflected God's truth. Whether the language used is mostly emotional (i.e., literature) or intellectual (i.e., philosophy), it is the soul's work to add to it the love of God in both heart and mind (Matt. 22:37). This facet of his development undoubtedly fed into his later reflection that loving God and loving one's neighbor is not a matter of the heart alone, but involves the selfless gift of the whole person to another.

His profound writings on love and marriage, in particular, emphasize how dividing human being into parts and imagining that one can love one's spouse in the heart, while not expressing that love through genuine acts of charity (with the hands), and reinforcing that belief in the mind, is one of the major reasons why many marriages have lost their joy. It also reflects, in turn, our difficulty in truly experiencing God's presence in our lives. After all, for John Paul II, human marriage was a sort of "primordial sacrament" intended to usher the first man and woman into communion with God's own way of love. By offering the selfless gift of one's whole self to one's spouse, and receiving the same gift of one's spouse in return, one begins to understand in a sacramental way the sort of relationship God created us to have with Him in the beginning.

Love demands the participation of the whole human being—not just one's heart. This love is comprehended in what John Paul II called the "hermeneutic of the gift." That is to say, the meaning of our lives is interpreted (thus, "hermeneutic") through the image of mutually giving and receiving a gift. One gifts one's whole self to another—usually a spouse, but for a priest it is the Church—and one gladly receives the gift of the other's whole self in turn. This receipt of the gift is what the New Testament defines as faith. Faith is not merely intellectual knowledge, nor is it pure emotion. Instead, it is a willingness of the whole self to receive the gift of God's very self to us—exemplified through the death and resurrection of Jesus and delivered to us through the sacraments. Thus, loving God meant, for the young seminarian, worshiping Him through an appreciation of both the literary arts and philosophy.

After the Black Sunday of 1944, a member of the reformist wing of the Polish nobility, the aging Archbishop Adam Stefan Sapieha, turned over his residence to the underground seminary. The home was crammed full of books and cots so that the few students who could study there would have a place to rest. Almost three years earlier, the archbishop had submitted a request to retire to Rome, but his request fell in the interim following the death of Pope Pious XI and went unanswered. Determined to dedicate whatever life he had left to ensuring that Poland was provided with a new generation of priests, he fearlessly welcomed Wojtyla and a handful of other candidates for the priesthood into his home. He declared to the students and faculty at their first meeting that if the Nazis discovered them, they should not fear but trust in God. "We will trust God's providence," he confidently declared, "[and n]o harm will befall us."

Wojtyla found the archbishop's faith and courage inspiring. This was not Sapieha's only act of defiance. He had also issued baptismal certificates to many of Krakow's Jews in an effort to protect them from the Nazis. Such an act, under normal circumstances, might be deemed heretical. In this context, however, it was justified as an act of love that covers all. This impressed upon the young seminarian that God's universal love extends beyond those who are within the official pale of the Catholic Church and that the love of God extends to all because human beings possess a dignity by virtue of God's loving act of creation. While the Jewish people rejected Jesus as their Christ, they were still human beings dignified by God's universal love.

Therefore, Jesus' command to love one's neighbor cannot be constrained to those who accept creedal Christianity. It extends to all people, even those who deny His existence and reject His grace. Love is carried out by the Christian according to God's role as creator. God remains the sole judge when it comes to salvation, but mankind is called to love, regardless, and not to limit love of one's neighbor according to one's presumption of God's eternal judgment on that neighbor. To love one's neighbor is not contingent on the neighbor's faith. Rather, faith is formed by love, and the Christian's embrace of God's universal love testifies to God's redemption in Christ.

# The Communist Occupation

When the Soviet Red Army marched upon Krakow in January 1945, the German occupiers were forced to retreat—though they did not leave quietly. They burned down the Debniki Bridge and smashed the archbishop's windows as they left. The SS had been occupying the old seminary near Wawel Castle, and when Wojtyla and his seminary's faculty moved to reclaim the facility, they found the place in disarray. Stained glass windows were shattered, and open fires had been used within the buildings to keep the place warm, which led to smoke damage throughout the facility. One of the tile roofs had collapsed. Even the pipes were frozen, and the toilets, which were likewise frozen with water and clogged with human excrement, had to be broken up and discarded. Wojtyla himself volunteered for this unpleasant task.

A return to a free Poalnd, however, was not to be. The exiled Polish government had granted the USSR complete control the year before in the event that they successfully overtook the German occupiers. Stalin himself had described the process of imposing communism upon Poland as like "fitting a cow with a saddle." Still, the Jagiellonian University and the Krakow seminary were able to resume business as normal under the communist regime, even as the Polish people continued to have many of their freedoms limited by a second totalitarian occupier.

Wojtyla began his final year of seminary studies in 1945 and also assumed a graduate position as a teaching assistant. He began considering his post-seminary vocation. On the one hand, he remained attracted to the Carmelite mystics and St. John of the Cross. He considered, with some angst, the possibility of entering a Carmelite monastery and devoting himself to a contemplative life. As stories of sainted martyrs under the Nazi regime began to circulate, however, Wojtyla felt an urge to pursue a life patterned after the martyrs—one whereby he might give of himself for the sake of others. He learned of a martyred Franciscan, Father Maximillian Mary Kolbe, who in the

Auschwitz starvation bunker willingly gave up his life to save another prisoner, a married man with children. The contemplative habit of the Carmelites, while honorable, would not satisfy this urge to follow a priestly call as one who willingly sacrifices oneself for others.

# Chapter Four: Wojtyla the Priest

# Ordination

Karol Wojtyla passed his ordination exams in July 1946. Yet, the former archbishop Sapieha—recently made a cardinal—was determined that Wojtyla should continue his education in pursuit of a doctorate at the Angelicum in Rome. If Wojtyla were to qualify to begin coursework for the fall 1946 semester, an accelerated ordination schedule was necessary. He was ordained as a priest the beginning of November and baptized an infant only days later, on November 11. He received a special invitation to attend a Rhapsodic Theater production later that month, by the same troupe he had helped form, which he gladly accepted. His priestly duties constrained him, however, and he was unable to attend an anniversary meeting of the troupe scheduled shortly thereafter. This does not mean that Wojtyla had abandoned his dreams of the theater. Instead, as a priest, he believed it was less an abandonment of the theater and more a reframing of his stage. He was assuming what he believed to be the greatest role he had ever played, that of an actor-priest, and he viewed his vocation as a mediation of God's truth to His people in a way that impacted every dimension of their lives.

As a priest and doctoral candidate, Wojtyla found himself traveling regularly. For the young Pole, who had never traveled outside of Poland until he went to Rome for doctoral studies, it was an enormously engaging and illuminating experience. With funds provided by Cardinal Sapieha, Wojtyla traveled around Europe in the summer of 1947. He later recalled several parts of that trip that left a lasting impression upon him. He went to France, where he met with several worker-priests in Paris and discussed the "enormously important" task of evangelizing the post-Christian French proletariat. He went to Belgium, where he spent the majority of the summer, and worked feverishly in a mission to Polish miners, hearing confessions and teaching the catechism.

Hearing confession became an important part of the young priest's ministry. During his travels, he saw firsthand how Europe was becoming de-Christianized, whether by the spread of secularism and the spirit of pessimism that befell Europe in the post-war era, or by the spread of communism, which regularly forbade free Christian thought and practice wherever it went. He believed that the battle against secularism was best fought in the confessional. It was easy to speak in generalities if preaching, but in the confessional, he found that he was able to speak to real people, addressing their real worries and doubts, and could speak to their guilt-panged consciences with an evangelical message that offered a hopeful way forward. To those under the communists' thumb, he could share his own experience under the Nazis and inspire them with tales of courage. He was convinced that the path toward revival in Europe would go through the confessional. Only by addressing God's people individually could a priest adequately speak to the problems that plagued their minds and troubled their souls.

# Doctoral Dissertation

Though Wojtyla had become engaged in mission work around Europe, when he returned to Rome, his primary task was to complete his doctoral dissertation. He had passed his master's exam in theology with a perfect score in July 1947, so the only thing that remained for his doctorate was a completed dissertation. Amongst the faculty at the Angelicum, Father Reginald Garrigou-Lagrange shared Wojtyla's fascination with Carmelite mysticism and the writings of St. John of the Cross. Thus, Father Garrigou-Lagrange naturally became Wojtyla's dissertation supervisor. Wojtyla's dissertation was written in Latin and, in translation, it was entitled *The Doctrine of Faith According to St. John of the Cross.*

In his dissertation, Wojtyla underscored that every human being's encounter with God is a personal one. Encountering God means transcending, but not forsaking, one's existence as a creature of God. It means becoming more truly human, as God first imagined humanity to be from the beginning, rather than escaping one's place in the world. The way one comes to know God, however, is not by merely acquiring knowledge or by engaging in intense contemplation, the sort of piety typically associated with the mystical tradition. One can't come to know God the same way one would know an inanimate object or a subject for study. Rather, one comes to know God the same way someone comes to know a person—through an act of mutual self-giving, as God gives himself to the Christian and the Christian responds by offering his own life to God in return.

Wojtyla also took aim at the spirit of modernity in his dissertation. Countering the notion that human reason is the key to discovering truth, he argued that God escapes the conventional pattern of scientific inquiry. God is not an object that can be dissected and examined, contained in a laboratory, and poked or prodded by the normal methods of acquiring knowledge. While one can rely on reason to make a case that God exists, reason does no more to bring one into a personal encounter with God than a history textbook might introduce someone to Abraham Lincoln.

Even faith, Wojtyla affirmed, does not allow human reason to make full sense of God. If that were the case, then human faith would be greater than His infinite nature. One can only know God through a personal encounter with Him, on account of His grace. Neither faith nor reason can master God—even though Wojtyla himself had earned a master's degree in theology, and on account of this dissertation, a doctorate in divinity as well—but faith and reason are *mastered by God* when we encounter Him personally.

Still, the nihilistic declaration of Nietzsche that "God is dead" did not surprise Wojtyla. If we knew a god to be wholly comprehensible by human reason, then it must be a dead god, or an idol. This is the defining characteristic of every false god: human beings create these idols, which therefore can do nothing more than what human beings declare possible. Thus, any argument that seeks to disprove God through human reason begs the question from the start. To make this kind of argument, one has to envision a limited god, whose nature and will wholly cohere to the canons of human reason. To set up this kind of false god, and then declare that he cannot exist, is a sort of elaborate tautology. Modernity, therefore, has not waged a war against God, but against idols. In this sense, Wojtyla could consider himself the product of modernity while also transcending it.

The indiscoverable nature of God, or what Wojtyla termed God's "non-objectifiability," should not trouble one's conscience in the least. Having witnessed irrational evil in his own life, Wojtyla found great comfort in God's mysterious transcendence. Only a God whose nature is beyond the rational is capable of rescuing us from our own irrational existence. Only a God who is a mystery in Himself can legitimately defy the incomprehensible evils of this age. For this reason, faith need never be shaken by insensible evil. Faith clings to a God who is greater than what we deem sensible. It is often when we are subjected to sufferings and evils in this world that don't "make sense" that we become acutely aware of our own limitations and the barrier between ourselves and God is broken down. When we recognize our insufficiency, God declares that His grace is sufficient for us (1 Corinthians 12:19).

In his dissertation, he also articulated his conviction, which he came to realize through his previous sufferings, that human beings possess an "inalienable dignity." Freedom is the pivotal point upon which human dignity stands. If one is going to experience a personal encounter with God, it occurs through a relationship of mutual self-giving. God freely gives Himself to us, and we freely give ourselves to Him in response. The modern era, Wojtyla believed, had reduced the human being to an economic unit, an expression of class or race, and valued the human being based on whatever he could produce. This, Wojtyla believed, ran contrary to the way God created man—dignified by a character that He granted human beings in creation and reinforced through redemption.

The themes Wojtyla engaged in his dissertation would echo throughout all his writings for the remainder of his life. Accordingly, these themes will not be elaborated upon again with the same detail. Rather, as these themes emerge to address a variety of conditions and situations, they will be evoked and rehearsed in order to demonstrate their vast utility for understanding the richness of Christian discipleship.

While Wojtyla received a perfect score on his oral defense of his dissertation, he did not receive his doctoral degree from the Angelicum. The rules there required that his work be published before the degree could be conferred, and as a priest who had assumed a vow of poverty with no family to help him foot the bill, he was unable to afford the printing costs necessary. Instead, he resubmitted his dissertation to the theology department at the Jagiellonian University, which conferred upon him his doctoral degree in theology in 1948.

# A Polish Priest

As he worked through the final stages of his dissertation, and was in the process of re-submitting it to the Jagiellonian University, Wojtyla received his first parish assignment in Niegowic, Poland, in July 1948. Less than a year later, he was reassigned to St. Florian's parish, where he apprenticed as a chaplain. Poland was under Soviet control, and while Wojtyla had hoped the conditions would be better than they had been under the Nazis, he was sadly disappointed. Blazynski described the state of Poland at the time as a place "where the dawn knock on the door was still expected, where prisons were full and beatings many, where the secret policeman was still his brother's keeper, and where the Great Teacher was neither Christ nor Buddha but the megalomaniac son of a Gregorian shoemaker through whom millions had died." No priest today faces a challenge any greater than Wojtyla did when he first began his priestly ministry.

The Soviets, while they despised the Nazis, nonetheless employed methods that reeked of the same totalitarianism. Priests were forbidden from engaging the nation's youth. The Soviets' atheism drove their agenda to sever Poland's rich history from its ties to Roman Catholicism.

On the one hand, the Polish Catholics were well accustomed to oppression. Having survived under the Nazi occupation, they emerged stronger and more committed to their faith than ever before. At the same time, however, the church was weakened. There were fewer priests, and since only a small number of Poles (Wojtyla included) had managed to make it through the underground seminary undetected, there were few new Polish priests available for placement in Poland's parishes. Wojtyla had learned, however, based on his own experience as a layman and by observing how other faithful laymen assumed a pious calling and served Christ under the Nazi threat, that the sanctity of a churchly vocation belonged to more than ordained priests. It was a calling that every Christian must assume.

In his first parish, Karol Wojtyla lived in poverty with few amenities. On one occasion, when an old woman in the parish had been robbed, he gave her the only pillow and comforter he had (one that some of the parishioners had just give him) while he chose to sleep on a bare slab.

While Wojtyla was modest with respect to his person, his plans were anything but. On the occasion of the senior priest's fiftieth anniversary, the parish members gathered to consider what they might do to surprise him. A few small projects were suggested, like painting the church or repairing a few things around the building—but Wojtyla suggested constructing a whole new church! He believed they had the capacity to raise the money and build it themselves. Many were shocked when his plan was a success. The church was well-built with brick and still stands and operates as an active parish to this day.

Though he was only at his first parish for eight months, apart from the impressive feat of constructing a new church, Wojtyla drew upon his past experiences and organized a drama club, which performed plays under his direction. He started a Living Rosary group and chose several young men to lead it. When the communist occupiers caught wind of the activities going on at the parish, they attempted to intimidate the Living Rosary group into disbanding—but the members refused. Wojtyla supposedly told them not to fret, remarking that the communists would eventually "finish themselves off."

In March 1949, Cardinal Sephiea transferred Wojtyla to a larger setting, where he believed the latter's talents could influence a greater number of the Polish faithful. St. Florian's church, just outside of Krakow, already had a senior pastor and three assistants. As a larger church, it was thriving but also a larger target for the Stalinist occupiers.

During a parish trip, accompanied by a number of young females (though priests were forbidden to interact with young women under Stalin), one of the girls asked Wojtyla what they should call him if asked. He bade them to call him "Wujek," or "Uncle." The nickname "Wujek" stuck, particularly amongst the youth at St. Florian's, and remained with him throughout his time there.

With the curriculum of Poland's universities strictly dictated by Stalinist restrictions, many of St Florian's faithful turned to Wojtyla, whose intellect and academic capacity offered an alternative to the strict secularism and atheism being taught elsewhere. For instance, he assigned a reading from Thomas Aquinas to some of his parish's young people, and asked them to discuss how Aquinas' concept of nature compared to what they were learning in their secular classrooms and labs. While Wojtyla had no formal training in the natural sciences, he recruited many to join his discussion groups, and it was observed that Wojtyla had an "instinctive" grasp of physics.

Especially given that he worked with so many young people, the prospect of marriage was a frequent topic of discussion. Rather than follow the tradition at the time of simply performing an examination and approving or disapproving a request for matrimony, Wojtyla established a whole course designed to prepare the couple for experiencing marriage after God's design—which for Wojtyla, was a way of experiencing God Himself. While such marriage preparation courses are a staple in parishes today, at that time in Poland, it was innovative.

In a letter to Terese Heydel, one of the members of his parish who was preparing for marriage, Wojtyla wrote that love "leads us outside ourselves to affirming others: devoting oneself to the accuse of man, to people, and above all, to God. Marriage makes sense ... if it gives one the opportunity for such love, if it evokes the ability and necessity of such loving, if it draws one out of the shell of individualism (various kinds) and egocentrism. It is not enough to want to accept such love. One must know how to give it, and it's often not ready to be received. Many times it's necessary to help it to be formed." And in a second letter to Miss Heydel, penned a month later, he declared, "I am convinced that the ... starting point of love is the realization that I am needed by another. The person who *objectively* needs me the most is also, for me, *objectively*, the person I most need."

Understood in this context, the sexual expression of love within marriage is deemed a holy and beautiful thing. Love bears fruit. When a married couple in his parish had a child, he would allow the family a day and then visit them the day after. At that time, he baptized the newborn child in the family's home. Because he believed that baptism means to "come home," he believed that baptizing infants within their homes was a powerful reflection of God's promise that His presence is our very home in this world.

While serving as a priest, Wojtyla continued his hobbies as a poet and playwright. One of his earliest plays, *The Jeweler's Shop,* told the story of three marriages, each challenged by unique circumstances. A constant theme that emerges is that love is not merely an emotion. The love of marriage, rather, is based on an eternal and moral truth. The stories told in *The Jewler's Shop* reveal how marriage is not based on our emotions, but it does transform them. It brings each couple into a relationship defined by self-giving love, which in turn draws them into the divine reality that marriage represents.

No matter the needs of his various parishioners, and whatever their age, Wojtyla took a pastoral strategy of "accompaniment," believing that the priest, like Jesus with His disciples, ministers to them as he walks alongside them through life. He was not a distant academic who lectured from a pulpit and disappeared, only to re-emerge when he had a class to teach or an ecclesiastical duty to perform. Instead, he took an active interest in whatever his parishioners were doing and did whatever he could to live among them, bearing their burdens and even getting his hands dirty with their labors.

This was linked, in fact, to his success as a father confessor. As stated before, Wojtyla viewed the confessional as a key battlefield, where spiritual warfare was fought head-on. Because Wojtyla walked alongside his parishioners, they perceived within him a "permanent openness" and a non-judgmental spirit that made them feel comfortable confessing their sins, and sharing their struggles and temptations, with their priest when going to confession.

# Bishop Wojtyla and Vatican II

On July 4, 1958, Pope Pious XII named Karol Wojtyla as auxiliary bishop of Krakow. The timing couldn't have been more important, as only a few months later, Pope John XXIII announced the Second Vatican Council (aka Vatican II). It also made him the youngest bishop in Poland, at the age of thirty-eight. In his role as bishop, Wojtyla stood by his often-quoted conviction that "the Church is not an organization of Christ, it is an organism of Christ." Thus, he did not view his elevation as a move toward an administrative role, but as an expansion of his pastorate. Shortly after being made bishop, some of his parishioners questioned how things might change. He simply replied, "Wujek will remain Wujek," invoking the nickname his parishioners had given him. And sure enough, even as bishop, he continued doing many of the tasks he had before, including a yearly kayaking trip with couples taking his marriage preparation course.

Before the Second Vatican Council opened in Rome, on October 11, 1962, Wojtyla received word that the communist authorities in Poland were attempting to seize Krakow's seminary buildings for use by their Higher School of Pedagogy. The young bishop set aside his plans in preparation for the council and made his way to Krakow. In an unprecedented move, he boldly demanded to speak with the secretary of the local Communist party. No meeting like this had ever occurred before, but he managed to negotiate a compromise in the seminary's favor. The Higher School of Pedagogy was granted space on the seminary's third floor, but the seminary retained the first two floors and administrative rights over the facility.

With the crisis at the Krakow seminary averted, Bishop Wojtyla left for Rome to take part in the impending council. This was a council unlike any other that had been held in the history of Christendom. Previously, councils were called in order to formalize doctrinal matters or refute heresies. As a result, the product of most councils had been creeds, canons, and condemnations. Pope John XXIII, however, had a different vision for this council. In the midst of the post-World War II years and the ongoing spread of communism throughout Europe and the world, Pope John hoped for a council that would be pastoral and evangelical in orientation, modeled more after the original Pentecost than Nicaea. It was intended to engage many of the same themes that Wojtyla had addressed for years, engaging the spirit of modernity with the Spirit of Christ and reaffirming the message of the gospel as an eternal hope that transcends the troubles of any time or place.

While Wojtyla was optimistic about these goals, many within the church remained skeptical that any dialogue or confrontation with modernity would set the church against powerful forces, not unlike the political forces of the French Revolution, that would lead to the collapse of Christendom. Many historians interpret Vatican II as an occasion to draw a dividing line between the church's "liberals" and "conservatives," with the former winning in spite of the latter's resistance. While this interpretation is not wholly off base or without merit, Bishop Wojtyla believed, as he would when he became Pope John Paul II, that this narrow interpretation missed the point, and the essential experience, of the council itself.

Bishop Wojtyla did not miss a single session of the Second Vatican Council, and he spoke on many issues, impressing many of the bishops and cardinals gathered. Arguably, it was at Vatican II that Wojtyla went from being a charismatic and powerful Polish bishop to being a bishop who belonged to all of the Church—whose voice began to have an impact on the broader Church at large. For Wojtyla, the council was above all else a spiritual experience, an "act of love" that stood in stark contrast to a hateful age, and a demonstration of the truth the Christians could still live in "full participation in divine truth" in the modern era.

Wojtyla was not naive about the political sects and dividing lines that had formed and were codified in Vatican II. He listened to and understood arguments from both sides of many issues—a fact that has continued to make John Paul II a difficult figure to easily classify as "liberal" or "conservative" in the usual way. As Wiegel succinctly put it, however, Wojtyla insisted that at Vatican II, the protagonist of the council's story was the Holy Spirit, not ecclesiastical factions.

A common theme that emerged in Wojtyla's writings and speeches at the council was an advocacy for methods and changes that prioritized effective teaching and evangelism. For instance, in the debate over liturgical renewal, Wojtyla presented reflections on his own experience, arguing that baptismal rites should place a greater emphasis on the parents' and godparents' responsibility for raising and instructing a child in the faith. He also emphasized the point that every baptized Christian is called to a vocation of holiness.

# Chapter Five: Archbiship of Krakow

# Vatican II

Karol Wojtyla began participating in the Second Vatican Council as a junior auxiliary bishop. By the time the third and fourth sessions of the council were held in 1964 and 1965, respectively, Wojtyla had been elevated to the position of archbishop of Karakow. Undoubtedly, the impressions he made at the council, in addition to his widely recognized influence in the Polish church, played a pivotal role in his rapid elevation.

The most controversial issue he addressed in the course of the council was religious freedom. Some at the council believed that once something was defined as an "error," it should enjoy no rights or protection by the state. Accordingly, it was argued, the ideal condition for the Church was to exist within a state that agreed with the Church's beliefs and defended it, privileging Christianity above other worldviews. Some argued, in turn, that if the Church embraced "religious freedom," it would amount to an endorsement of secular worldviews. On the opposite side of this argument were the American bishops who, accustomed to living under the separation of church and state, believed that history had shown Christianity to be guaranteed more security under freedom of religion than in European-style governments, which could just as easily turn against Christianity as endorse it.

Archbishop Wojtyla, however, addressed the issue in different terms. For Wojtyla, many of the arguments being made failed to understand the fundamental nature of freedom. Freedom is not merely freedom *from* something, or freedom set *against* a particular threat or worldview. Instead, freedom is properly understood as freedom *for* the truth. Religious freedom is necessary because one can only live in the truth if one is free to do so. Under a government that supports Christian principles or endorses the Church's institutions, there is not real freedom because one can never be sure whether one's adherence to the faith is maintained out of sincerity or compulsion. Taking his definition of freedom as a freedom *for,* he drew two conclusions: (1) The state is not a competent interpreter of theology and has no business deciding ecclesiastical or theological matters. (2)

The communist argument that religion "alienated" people, and was therefore a legitimate target of the state—i.e., it is legitimate to oppress those whom one deems to be part of an oppressive force—was simply wrong. Human beings are not alienated by true religion; they are completed by it.

Also connected to Wojtyla's conviction for religious freedom was his theology and faith in divine revelation. God's truth is not simply one amongst many competing in a marketplace of ideas. The truth of God is latent with power, convincing in its own right. Religious freedom need not be feared if someone believes that the truths of Christianity are inherently true and capable of changing hearts and minds on their own. False beliefs, including heresies, other religions, or secular ideas, do not threaten divine truth because their foundation rests on human invention and reason, whereas the gospel is discerned from divine revelation. If one is confident in this belief, error itself is not the grave threat that the Church had sometimes treated it as. While error should be taken seriously, error does not cohere with a power that in any way endangers the integrity of the truth of God's Word.

Ultimately, Vatican II decided the issue in favor of Wojtyla's arguments. The council produced *Dignitatis Humanae* (The Dignity of Humanity), which unequivocally stated:

> The Vatican Council declares that the human person has a right to religious freedom. Freedom of this kind means that all men should be immune from coercion on the part of individuals, social groups, and every human power so that, within due limits, nobody is forced to act against his convictions in religious matters in private or in public, alone or in association with others. The Council further declares that the right to religious freedom is based on the very dignity of the human person as known through the revealed word of God and by reason itself. This right of the human person to religious freedom must be given such recognition in the

constitutional order of society as will make it a civil right.

The contribution to Vatican II for which Archbishop Karol Wojtyla is best known is what was later called the *Pastoral Constitution on the Church in the Modern World. Schema XIII.* In what is arguably his most famous speech given at the council, Wojtyla argued that the world should not be viewed as something "other" than the church, and certainly not as an essential enemy of the church. Nor is the biblical story of creation and redemption something other than the world's story. Creation and redemption are not things that happens to occur within the world; they are the story of the world's very existence and destiny. The biblical story *is* the world's story. The closer one comes to God, the closer one comes to true humanity and the truth of the world.

Therefore, the message that the Church should proclaim into the modern world is that the Christian faith is not alienating—to the contrary, it is the most liberating message ever articulated because it is the only message that speaks to human liberty derived from the innate dignity of human beings made in God's image. Elsewhere, Wojtyla summarized this particular document, and the point of the council at large, as follows: "It is only in the mystery of the Word made flesh that the mystery of man truly becomes clear … [and] all this holds true, not for Christians only, but also for all men of good will in whose hearts grace is actively present."

During the course of the council, Wojtyla was concerned that its proceedings not remain in ivory towers. Whenever he could, he returned to Poland and communicated the significance of the council's actions to the laypeople in a way that was meaningful to their daily lives. With regard to the *Pastoral Constitution on the Church in the Modern World. Schema XIII*, Wojtyla put pen to paper and enshrined many of the ideas he had emphasized at the council, but he added both a stronger philosophical foundation and a more accessible way of explaining it so that the ideas of the council could speak to the layperson as well as to the intelligentsia of the day. He entitled the work he produced *Person and Act.*

In *Person and Act*, Wojtyla laid out what might be deemed the ethical or moral dimension of human personhood. While modernity pressed an idea of freedom that emphasized radical self-autonomy and self-assertion, Wojtyla insisted that it is *self-mastery* that truly leads to human freedom. This self-mastery is not a matter of simply repressing human passions and desires, but of channeling normal human impulses of both body and mind into actions that deepen one's humanity, conforming the person to things as they truly are—as God intended them to be.

To illustrate Wojtyla's point, one need only think of how addicts might defend their "autonomous" right to indulge in alcohol, drugs, sex, gambling, or any other addictive behavior. But exercising one's autonomy toward something that is destructive to one's welfare and is contrary to the good life God intends for us is not a freedom at all; it is a form of bondage or a slavery. Because freedom is an essential component of what it means to be human, freedom is experienced when we live the human lives God designed for us to live in the beginning. Thus, the married person may not feel "free" to commit adultery or act on any passion or impulse, but the married person is free when, through self-mastery, he or she learns to channel those passions in a way that builds up the marriage and, therefore, puts one into close contact with God's self-giving love. Freedom is not a matter of having no restraints—freedom is a matter of living in the fullness of how one was created to live.

Experience proves Wojtyla's point. The same point, in fact, was discerned by King Solomon, as evidenced in the book of Proverbs. How many people who live truly righteous lives, who are disciplined and do not indulge in sinful behaviors, are unhappy? In truth, those who live according to God's ethic tend to be very happy people. Conversely, how many people who indulge the flesh, who turn to addictions or are sexually promiscuous, are satisfied with their lives? Very few people are depressed who live in the freedom of God's design for life, aside from those who are depressed in a clinical sense and/or as a result of chemical imbalances. Self-mastery leads to godliness and happiness. Self-assertion, unbridled, leads to unhappiness and trouble in this life.

# Poland's Bishop

Karol Wojtyla was only forty-three years old when Cardinal Wyszynski made him archbishop of Krakow. He was the seventy-sixth bishop to hold the seat, going all the way back to the earliest days of Poland's origins, in the kingdom of the Piasts. How Karol Wojtyla ended up being made archbishop at such a young age, having only been a bishop at all for a short amount of time, is an intriguing tale. Based on an agreement between the Catholic Church and Poland's communist regime made in 1956, the process for choosing a new archbishop required that the Roman Primate submit a list of nominees chosen by the Holy See to the government. The government, in turn, had veto power. They could veto any nominee put forward, or simply fail to respond, in which case the nominee could be elevated within three months' time.

Apparently, the Polish communist authorities had rejected candidate after candidate. Zenon Kliszko—the authority who carried most of the decision power in this regard in the Polish government—allegedly vetoed seven names over the course of a year and a half. On one occasion, he wrote back to the Primate, "I'm waiting for Wojtyla, and I'll continue to veto names until I get him."

Knowing what we know about Wojtyla, both from his past and based on the life he subsequently led, it might seem odd that the communist regime would request Wojtyla. From their perspective, however, a young man in his forties who seemed to be an academic with little interest in politics seemed to be the ideal candidate, whom they believed could be easily manipulated and intimidated. How could the communist government have made such a serious miscalculation as advocating for Wojtyla to become archbishop? They likely knew of his impassioned rhetoric and his deep piety. They knew he was a powerful and effective religious communicator. But under the communist ideology, religion was merely "opium," and true power came through strength of arms. They did not see how his rhetoric on religious freedom translated into resistance against communist control. In this, they couldn't have been more wrong!

How little time it took to realize their blunder is illustrated by a series of communications from the warden at the prison in Gdansk, where Father Piotr Rostworowsky was being held for his role smuggling Czech citizens across the Czech–Polish border. On account of the priest's capture, tensions were high between Rome and the Polish government. When Wojtyla was elevated, the warden supposedly gloated to the prisoner that this was "very good news" because Wojtyla was precisely the man whom "the comrades wanted." Four months later, the same warden cried, "Wojtyla has swindled us!" Karol Wojtyla proved to be a staunch advocate for the Polish people and a powerful opponent of the communist regime, which grossly miscalculated when advocating for his elevation. In spite of communist opposition, from 1962 until 1978, the Archdiocese of Krakow under Wojtyla's leadership established an impressive eleven new parishes, with ten more "pastoral centers" that were effectively parishes in the making.

Since canon law forbade the formation of new parishes without a church building, the government's tactic to thwart the growth of the church was simply to deny building permits. Wojtyla was persistent, filing an average of thirty building permit requests each year, which resulted in a backlog of requests that remained unanswered. In addition, skirting the boundaries of what canon law required, Wojtyla along with several priests established unofficial house-churches through door-to-door evangelism. When the gatherings proved too large, Wojtyla would petition the authorities again, insisting that the church already existed and that preventing them from having a building would leave them with no alternative but to conduct services on the streets or in public facilities—a prospect that the regime deemed riskier than "containing" the parishes within their own dedicated buildings. In addition, with such a backlog of permits, he argued that he would be willing to withdraw a majority of his requests if only one were granted. While he had never intended to use so many buildings, he presented it in such a way that it appeared he was giving up more than he was requesting. More often than not, Wojtyla was successful in manipulating the regime to approve new permits.

In a pastoral letter for Lent, 1964, the newly elevated archbishop wrote to each parish within his jurisdiction that to serve as their archbishop meant a "profound sense of responsibility" furthered by the "great and eloquent memories of the past." He also wrote that, as their bishop, he saw himself as only "the first servant" of the common good and expected every Christian whom he served to take "responsibility for that part which the will of God has given him." These kinds of reflections were common, even while serving as a parish priest. This showed, however, that Wojtyla continued to view himself not as holding a place of privilege on account of his ecclesiastical title, but as servant. In fact, the higher his title in the ecclesiastical hierarchy, the more he believed he was duty-bound as a servant to God's people and the world.

# Cardinal Wojtyla

In total, Karl Wojtyla served as the archbishop of Krakow for fourteen years, though only four years after he became an archbishop, Pope Paul VI made him a cardinal. When he became a cardinal, his interests were expanded beyond the concerns of his archdiocese and he became a more high-profile representative of the Church throughout the world. In August and September of 1969, he made his first trip to Canada and the United States, visiting a number of prominent parishes. After his visit to the United States, particularly in the post-Vietnam era, he became concerned that the U.S. had viewed the crisis of freedom that the world was experiencing as one that involved a binary choice between democracy and communism. He was also concerned that many Americans, who had lived their lives without their liberty in serious peril, had come to think of liberty in terms of license and took their freedom for granted. The great crisis facing the world was not a matter of democracy versus communism; it was a confrontation between the Church and the anti-Church—it was about the dignity of human beings. Communism was one of the world's greatest threats to human freedom, as Wojtyla knew from human experience, but the answer was not democracy. The answer, rather, was a more thorough embrace of human dignity as experienced only through a personal encounter with God.

In spite of his growing worldwide influence, however, the bulk of his efforts and his heart remained with the Polish people. He became well-known amongst Polish Catholics for his charismatic and persuasive sermons accompanying the Corpus Christi processions. On June 10, 1971, he proclaimed from the fourth station altar, "We are the citizens of our country, the citizens of our city, but we are also a people of God which has its own Christian sensibility… We will continue to demand our rights. They are obvious, just as our presence here is obvious. We will demand!" He echoed similar sentiments during his Corpus Christi processional sermons for several years thereafter, declaring in 1978, "A nation … has a right to the truth about itself." This truth, of course, was Poland's long historical tradition, which included Polish nationalism and Polish Catholicism as two sides of a single coin.

During his time as Krakow's archbishop, Cardinal Wojtyla also expended considerable energy reforming the seminary serving the Archdiocese of Krakow. It was one thing to train priests; it was another thing to prepare priests to become pastors. In other words, performing the official responsibilities of the priesthood required very little education or understanding. To administer the required rites takes little talent and requires little understanding of human experiences. To be a pastor, however, means being both a priest and an effective counselor—someone who, like Christ, walks alongside his people. Between 1962 and 1978, the seminary went from 191 students to 250, and the number of priests in the diocese increased from 771 to 956.

Wojtyla placed considerable emphasis on youth and family ministry and expanded his own yearlong course for marriage preparation to the seminary, as a component of training future priests/pastors, and throughout the parishes of his archdiocese. He did not hesitate to address controversial social issues, even conducting conferences on ministering to women who were healing from post-abortion stress. While he was a vigorous pro-life advocate, he also believed that those who had abortions should never be alienated by the Church. It is often in the wake of our darkest moments that the light of Christ shines the brightest.

After 1950, the communist regime in Poland outlawed all charitable institutions and organizations. Wojtyla was not dissuaded, and would not allow the Church to be reduced to a social club or inwardly focused sect. If the Church could not operate its own charitable organizations, then the focus needed to shift away from institutionalized charity to personal charity. The answer required a renewed vigor of parish life and a Christian's personal piety. Informal "charity teams" emerged as like-minded Catholics banded together to informally provide food, medicine, clothing, nursing care to the elderly, and home visitations for the neediest persons and families in the community. The communists, he reasoned, might be able to erect external barriers around the institutional dimension of the Church, but they could not effectively build walls around human hearts, compelled by the gospel to live charitable lives.

As a leader, Cardinal Wojtyla was known for his humility. Those deemed his subordinates were given considerable leeway, and he trusted them within their various spheres of responsibility. He strove to maintain an open mind, and he was not beyond persuasion if someone could give him a reason to change his mind over a position he had initially embraced. He welcomed and even expected his subordinates to offer constructive criticism in his leadership. He trusted them, which meant that they trusted him in return. If something his archdiocese produced was criticized, and he saw merit in the critique, Wojtyla readily accepted responsibility for any shortcomings and protected his subordinates from public scrutiny.

Sometimes, however, his "middle ground" approach frustrated other church leaders. In the wake of Vatican II, a debate erupted amongst the priests in his diocese regarding whether, under the revised liturgy, the Eucharist should be received kneeling, as was customary, or standing, which the new rites permitted. The advocates of either position quickly coalesced into their own respective parties, and the conflict became bitter. Cardinal Wojtyla listened quietly to the arguments on both sides. He allowed each priest the occasion to speak and defend his position. Once the sizzling emotions settled, Wojtyla approached the podium to declare his position, speaking clearly: "It seems that there are two positions."

The idea that each side could easily tolerate diversity in practice simply hadn't occurred to them, and his middle-ground approach, which saw merit in either position, helped assuage the tempers that were creating an unnecessary division in the archdiocese. None of the arguments posed by either side was worth embracing to the exclusion of the other if Christian unity was the cost of deciding the matter one way or the other.

# Humanae Vitae

While Wojtyla was adept at moderating disputes amongst his priests, the real test of his mettle as a mediator came with the controversy surrounding Pope Paul VI's 1968 encyclical, *Humanae Vitae.* Published in the midst of what secularists hailed as the "sexual revolution," the encyclical was written to address a number of controversial positions, particularly the church's traditional position on birth control. Pope Paul VI had called a commission to report on the question.

The majority report, representing a more liberal view, argued that either chemical (i.e., birth control pills) or mechanical (i.e., condoms and IUDs) were acceptable ways to prevent pregnancy insofar as these methods were used within a couple's overall openness to having children. The minority report, however, rejected contraception according to any means other than by following the natural rhythms of fertility. When Pope Paul VI released *Humanae Vitae*, which rejected the majority report and declared that "we must again insist that the interruption of the generative processes already begun must be totally rejected as a legitimate means of regulating the number of children," a widespread controversy erupted across Christendom.

Archbishop Wojtyla (not yet a cardinal), whose opinion the pope desired on account of his admiration of Wojtyla's *Love and Responsibilty*, was unable to attend the 1966 meeting where the majority opinion was written. The Polish government denied his passport, declaring that he had waited too long to reply. Accordingly, Wojtyla established a commission of his own within his archdiocese to debate the matter. Since he had been unable to contribute to the opinions made at Rome, Wojtyla sent the conclusions drawn by his own commission to Pope Paul VI. The Krakow theologians, following Wojtyla's lead, found both the minority and majority opinions in Rome to be deficient.

On the one hand, the minority opinion offered weak justification for why the use of a mechanical or chemical method introduces moral problems somehow more serious than preventing conception through the use of "natural family planning." In their estimation, to take such a controversial position on such flimsy theological ground was not likely to resolve the controversy. In turn, the majority opinion, which suggested that the morality of a single act of intercourse should be examined "proportionally" within the total context of marriage, was in the Krakow theologians' estimation an argument made without any grounding in moral theology, and it misread the biblical expression of human sexuality.

Accordingly, Archbishop Wojtyla and the Krakow theologians believed that the moral argument, which ultimately supported the position taken in *Humanae Vitae*, needed a new starting point. In order to examine the issue, one must first consider the nature of the human person since only human beings, amongst all God's creatures, are capable of morality. Human beings are not, in their moral nature, disembodied souls. Rather, the human being was declared "good" by God as a body-soul unity. To think as a moral being requires considering the whole person. Therefore, as the Krakow theologians argued, there is a "moral language" or "moral grammar" innate within the sexual structure of the human body. This moral language means that sexual intercourse should be considered within the realm of two moral questions: sex is (1) an expression of love and (2) a way for bearing the fruit of love through procreation. Intercourse understood in any other way, such as an act of pleasure alone (not that sex cannot be pleasurable, but pleasure in itself ought to be a means toward one of the two previous ends rather than an end unto itself) reduces one's spouse and even one's own body to an object to be exploited for the sake of the other's pleasure. Spousal love, rather, involves an act of mutual self-giving, as one donates the self to the other and receives the other in kind. In this way, human sexuality is defined within the human character by its openness to the possibility of resulting in a new life.

Decisions regarding procreation, however, were not necessarily left up to however many children one might produce before the woman's fertility fades. Rather, couples have the duty to plan their family with dignity, in "a dialogue of love between husband and wife," in a way that respects human dignity. This means upholding a cooperation of the spouses and respecting an equal right exhibited by the male and female when it comes to sexual procreation. The Krakow theologians argued that contraceptives violate these criteria by placing the burden for regulation upon the woman while freeing the man for hedonistic behavior without responsibility. Family planning, in turn, is the only method that respects nature's rhythms and emerges from a dialogue of love that gives male and female an equal role in the moral responsibility associated with procreation.

While the Krakow memorandum had an influence on *Humanae Vitae,* the encyclical ultimately failed to articulate the importance of human personhood in a way as persuasive or as thorough as Wojtyla's commission had done. Instead, the encyclical devoted a significant amount of space to addressing specific sexual acts, opening the encyclical to criticisms of "legalism" or "biologism," while also practicing out-of-touch pastoral insensitivity that neglected the real-world experiences of couples. While the Krakow memorandum more robustly defended the dignity of the human person, and the dignity of women in particular, the encyclical did not sufficiently elaborate on these points.

# Chapter Six: The Election of John Paul II

# The September Papacy

The tumult of the late 1960s continued in the 1970s as the divisions in society seemed to find their way into the Church. The backlash against *Humanae Vitae* had entrenched Catholic "conservatives" and "liberals" in extreme positions, widening the gulf between the parties and threatening the unity of the Church. In addition to the ongoing battle over contraception, disputes regarding papal authority, the celibacy of priests, and the ordination of women to the priesthood exacerbated rifts in the Church. In some regions of the world—particularly in Latin America, where the Church lived within authoritarian regimes—it was argued that Karl Marx could do for theology in the twentieth century what Aquinas had done in the thirteenth century.

The College of Cardinals elected Cardinal Albino Luciani of Venice as Pope John Paul I in August of 1978. On September 29, 1978, the newly elected pope was found dead in his bed. Cardinal Wojtyla received word shortly after returning to Krakow from what he'd thought was a successful conclave. By all appearances, it had been.

Pope Paul VI's death was not a surprise, on account of his ill health and old age. While he was widely loved, there was also a recognition that the Church was more divided than it had been in centuries at the end of Paul VI's life. The majority of the cardinals believed that they needed a strong-minded pope, committed to the Church's traditions, who could bring stability to the Church. In order to elect a new pope, however, it required a two-thirds majority plus one of the cardinal electors. With so many divisions amongst them, a quick conclave seemed unlikely. Though little is known about the conclave itself, due to the fact that these conclaves are guarded by an oath of secrecy, it appears that Pope Paul VI's assistant, Cardinal Giovannia Benelli of Florence, played a pivotal role in rallying support behind Cardinal Albino Luciani. He was elected on the fourth ballot on the first day of voting, making it the fastest conclave since the election of Pius XII in 1939.

Apparently, however, Pope John Paul I had some health problems, too, including a cardiovascular condition that had been diagnosed recently. Many believe that his unfamiliarity with the Church's bureaucracy added to his stress during his first and only month as pope, resulting in his fatal heart attack at the end of September. When Cardinal Wojtyla returned to Krakow, he was greeted by a crowd holding a banner declaring, "Wujek will remain Wujek." Upon receiving the news of Pope John Paul I's death, however, he began making preparations to have his duties delegated amongst his bishops.

Before leaving, Cardinal Wojtyla went on a leisurely hike with one of his assistants, Jerzy Jani, and his wife. As the couple recalled later, the wife asked Wojtyla, "Where shall we go when you become pope?" She remembers being surprised that he did not even laugh—suggesting to some that he had likely received a few votes in the previous election and did not think his election was altogether a wild stretch of the imagination. Instead, he told her, "We'll go to the Alps of the Apennines." To them, it meant that Wujek would remain Wujek, even if the "Uncle" should become "Papa."

# Setting the Stage

During the previous conclave, there had been some discussion about electing a non-Italian pope. Though the conclaves are sworn to secrecy, there were a number of information leaks, particularly as the August 1978 conclave was the first to receive such intense media scrutiny. There are always those who attempt to make predictions about the next pope while a conclave is ongoing, too, and many sentiments from the conclave were released, providing fodder for television's talking heads. Many had suggested that a non-Italian pope might be needed to help heal the factions in the Church. Some also took the shortened papacy of John Paul I as a sign that it might be time to look outside of Italy.

The problem was discerning where to look. A Western European was not likely to emerge from the new conclave, for the Church was more divided there than anywhere else in the world and no leader had emerged from amongst the cardinals to heal the divide effectively. Some thought that a pope from the Third World was a possibility, but it seemed as if this were more likely in the distant future and too removed from the current European problem to address the Church's need at the time. Almost no one considered an American pope as a possibility. While the American cardinals were influential, they looked at the world differently than the rest, and they also seemed to be too divided, like their Western European counterparts.

Cardinal Wojtyla was a European, but a European "from another world"—from the Polish Church that had uniquely thrived under the harshest regimes in the twentieth century. It was an intellectual church, and Cardinal Wojtyla had shown himself a capable voice when speaking to the challenges of modernity in a way that, while faithful to the Church's traditions, still seemed new and fresh. Polish Catholicism, likewise, had garnished the intrigue of many Western Christians due to its deep and popular piety—a feature that the Church in most of the West sorely lacked.

Wojtyla also had a reputation for mediating disputes. His contribution to *Humanae Vitae,* while not adequately contained in the encyclical itself, nonetheless formed a new way of reasoning that those on either side of the contraception debate found intriguing. He had successfully mediated a number of delicate exchanges between the Polish and German bishops. In addition, communism remained a major threat to the growing church in South America and the Third World, and Wojtyla had demonstrated to the world how, in spite of being under the Stalinist thumb, Catholicism could grow and thrive.

While all of these factors made Wojtyla a prime candidate to replace Pope John Paul I, many recognized that he did not have the usual disposition of a pope. He had little interest in the Church's bureaucratic processes, and he had an emotional connection to Krakow, where he believed his country remained in need of his leadership. In spite of these things, Wojtyla's name appeared amongst the top three on the first day of voting, October 15.

As the votes continued to be taken, it was clear that the two leading Italian candidates were in a deadlock, with few who favored each candidate willing to move to the other. In turn, both parties shifted and elected Karol Wojtyla on the eight ballot at the end of the second day of the conclave, October 16. He was the first non-Italian pope in 455 years.

Cardinal Ratzinger, amongst the youngest popes present, who would follow Pope John Paul II as Pope Benedict XVI, later remembered the conclave that elected the Church's first Polish pope. He recalled that the shock of September, particularly when so many were convinced that they had chosen God's man, led to a second conclave that was much more prayerful than the first. They were open to "the possibility of doing something new," and Wojtyla's election was the result.

Accounts of Wojtyla's election that have since leaked suggest that when the vote tallies came in, making it clear that Wojtyla was going to be elected, the young Polish cardinal simply put his head in his hands and prayed. This was not a joyous occasion, but a solemn one. Cardinal Hume recalled feeling "desperately sad for the man" who was about to be cut off from his previous life, with no chance of ever returning. Cardinal Koenig, who was the leading voice advancing Wojtyla's candidacy, recalled that when he saw how struck to the soul Wojtyla was, he was "very anxious about whether he would accept."

There are two ritual questions posed to a newly elected candidate for the papacy that he must answer before the white smoke will be released to signal the election of the new pope to the public. First, he is asked if he will accept the responsibility laid upon him. Wojtyla responded, in Latin, a somber "*accepto.*" Then, to the second question, which asked by what name he wished to be known, he indicated that—on account of his devotion to Paul VI and his affection for John Paul I—he would assume the name John Paul II.

# Chapter Seven: The Pope as Pastor and Evangelist

# A Pope from Galilee

Even as Poland erupted in tears of joy and celebration, declaring that "Wujek" had become Pope, the world's media responded in surprise. They focused not on his past and the reasons why he was elected, but on the novelty of electing a non-Italian pope. This, the world media thought, was a sign that the Church was adapting to the modern world. Yet, one French journalist who had done his homework declared in his newspaper, "This is not a Pope from Poland; this is a Pope from Galilee."

William Shakespeare famously declared that all of the world is a stage. In the mind of this young pope, who still had a passion for the theater, he had become the leading actor in the story of God that had reached its climax in Jesus of Nazareth. Now, as the Lord's chief representative on earth, it was his highest and most important task to represent the Person of Jesus Christ in the most important role he had ever played.

In spite of his relative youth, Pope John Paul II made it clear from the start that he was not going to be a puppet of the Curia. He defined any attempt to "tame" him or manage his unique approach to the papacy. During his first press conference, he broke all precedent and walked through the crowd of journalists to field impromptu questions, which he answered in English, Italian, French, Polish, and German. He was determined to lead "from below," as the first servant of the world, rather than dictate decrees from above. He believed that leading the Church in the modern world meant a new, pastoral and evangelical style that no pope of recent memory had practiced. Moreover, he stubbornly refused to take sides based on old divisions, but instead constantly declared truths to reframe old debates in ways that had yet to be considered. He made new, unconventional, appointments.

Though he considered himself a leader "from below," this sort of leadership (which people today call servant-leadership) was not a matter of weakness, but of leadership marked by strength. He was a servant to Christ, and as such, he was a leader in the Church—so no human authority or Curia could micromanage him. Like Jesus, who was a servant of all but also taught with authority, John Paul II reflected these dual truths in a way that was profound and winsome. While his ascension troubled many, particularly the Italians, who were less enthusiastic than the rest of the world about having a non-Italian pope, his unique approach to leading the Church eventually won most of them over.

# Changing the World

The Soviets, in particular, were unsettled by the election of John Paul II. Not only was his election a threat to the stability of the Soviet regime in Poland, which was the site of the Warsaw Pact and served as a bridge to East Germany, but also in Ukraine, where the Eastern-Rite Greek Catholic Church had been regularly persecuted from the time of Stalin, his election and his open opposition to communism risked igniting the flame of Ukrainian nationalism.

Of course, Pope John Paul II did not have any particular plan for attacking or dismantling the Soviet Union. That, he believed, was a role other political actors around the world might play. His role, rather, was to proclaim the eternal truth regarding the human condition expressed in the gospel. This truth, he believed, would necessarily butt heads with communism due to the truth of human nature and human community cohering in the truth of Jesus Christ. Likewise, he did not outright condemn Marxism and avoided attacking any particular communist regime. Still, his emphasis on human rights—especially the right of religious freedom—consistently undermined the core tenants of communism.

In his early years, the pope did not shy away from entering into many of the problems that the Church faced around the world. He went to Mexico in 1979, kissing the ground upon his arrival. In Mexico, in particular, the debate within the Church centered on how the post-Vatican II Church would engage "liberation theology."

While it is difficult to paint liberation theology with a single brush, fundamentally, it represented a more aggressive and revolutionary approach to reform than Vatican II, which had favored a gradual transformation of the world's social and economic structures advanced through the Christian's dialogue with the modern world. Advocates of liberation theology, further, believed that the Church should commit itself to openly "partisan" agendas, even if that meant positioning the "people's church" against the "hierarchal church." In Latin America, in particular, where the Church had been ineffective in empowering the poor, liberation theologies were popular and tended to see the world less in terms of "believers" and "unbelievers," but instead as separated between social and economic classes—between the "haves" and the "have-nots." Catholic renewal, therefore, had to be a bottom-up movement, which was a proposition with which John Paul II agreed and that he had, in fact, embraced in his own pastoral strategy in Krakow.

In his usual way, Pope John Paul II found what he could leverage within the tenets of liberation theology but refined it in a way that colored the agenda with a more evangelical bent. On the one hand, liberation theologies emerged from a legitimate complaint: oppression, whether it be economic or political or religious, was a worldwide problem. On the other hand, liberation by "any means necessary" often turned the oppressed into oppressors. John Paul II could not embrace the Marxist leanings of some liberation theologians and instead insisted that true liberation must be pursued in the manner exemplified by Jesus Himself. For those in the Church, their task was to teach the truth of Jesus Christ, the foundation of true liberation. Liberation theologians who viewed Jesus as a political revolutionary involved in class struggles failed to take into account the fact that Jesus loved everyone, and His love of the poor came from a universal love rather than a favoritism of one social class above another. Liberation in Jesus Christ comes through transformation, through peacemaking and unifying people of all stripes under the single banner of the gospel, through forgiveness, and in love that reconciles all human divisions.

Marxism, therefore, did not provide Christians with the sort of liberation that the human spirit requires. The Marxist error fails to account for the dignity of human beings made in God's image, and the "complete truth about the human being" is not one that divides people into victims and victimizers. People are not the victims of historic, political, or economic forces. As human beings liberated by the gospel, godly men and women seek justice in the world as artisans of new societies, economies, and politics that honor human dignity. In one of his first encyclicals, published in March 1979, entitled *Redemptor Hominis* or *The Redeemer of Man*, he introduced the world to his profoundly biblical view of the human person, insisting that "through he Incarnation ... God gave human life the dimension he had intended man to have from his first beginning."

When Jesus took human form in Bethlehem and went about living his life amongst sinful people, He revealed truths both about Himself and about human beings. The Son of God communicated "the fatherhood of God," which embraced the dignity and value of every human person and declared that "man cannot live without love... His life [remains] senseless, if love is not revealed to him, if he does not encounter love, if he does not experience it and make it his own, if he does not participate intimately in it." Love is greater than sin or any force that alienates man in the world (including sociological cr economic forces, political regimes, or prejudices). Because God is love (1 John 4:8), it is only by encountering God perscnally that the alienating forces in the world can be overcome. The answer to the world's problems is not a political revolution. It is a direct encounter with God, whose love conquers all.

# Going Home

For more than a millennium, Polish Christianity had thrived. In a few short years, the Communist regime's intention to re-frame Polish history in its own image failed to overcome the tides of history. When Pope John Paul II traveled to Poland in 1979, speaking in Victory Square, there was little the government could do to prevent "Wujek" from returning to his people. His ascension to the chair of St. Peter had inspired an even greater Catholic fervor in Poland, and the Communist regime knew it was ill-equipped to stand in the way.

Never in Polish history had Warsaw seen a crowd as large as that which greeted Pope John Paul II when he arrived on June 2, 1979. The usually gray city had been decorated with whatever colorful homemade decorations the people could muster. More than 300,000 Poles crammed into Victory Square, with nearly a million more filling the surrounding streets.

The message Pope John Paul II preached is often regarded as the greatest sermon he ever gave. He posed the question: Why had a Polish cardinal been elevated to the chair of St. Peter? He was convinced that, on account of the great sufferings Poland had endured through the twentieth century, Poland had been refined by fire and had become "the land of a particularly responsible witness." Together, the Polish people must stand together "to read again the witness of his cross and resurrection." The Poles' endurance testified to the fact that human beings possess an inherent dignity, one that "cannot be fully understood without Christ"—as, indeed, "man is incapable of understanding himself fully without Christ. He cannot understand who he his, nor what his true dignity is, nor what his vocation is, nor what his final end is. He cannot understand any of this without Christ."

For this reason, the attempt to silence the voice of Christ in Poland and the rest of the world was destined to fail. "The exclusion of Christ from the history of man is an act against man... The history of the [Polish] nation is above all the history of people. And the history of each person unfolds in Jesus Christ.

In him it becomes the history of salvation." He concluded his homily with a poetic prayer that he had penned himself:

> Let your Spirit descend.
> Let your Spirit descent.
> and renew the face of the earth,
> the face of this land. Amen.

In response, the crowd erupted with a chant: "We want God! We want God! We want God!"

Never before, aside from Peter's own Pentecost sermon, had a single homily changed so many hearts and minds. Poland could no longer be thought of as a communist nation. Instead, it was a Catholic nation under communism's attack—an attack destined to fail. This event became widely known as Poland's "second baptism." By unsettling one of the linchpins of communism, this single homily, many believe, pulled the first string that initiated the unraveling of the Soviet Union. In the subsequent years, which saw the final decline and fall of the USSR that culminated in 1990–1991, Pope John Paul II was one of the most influential voices. His role in undermining the philosophical failures of communism was rivaled by none. Along with the United States' President Ronald Reagan, Pope John Paul II played a crucial part in whittling away at the Soviet regime. What President Reagan accomplished politically, Pope John Paul II accomplished in the hearts and minds of the people—not only among the citizens of the USSR, but throughout the world.

# A Second Act?

Many have observed that Pope John Paul II's life consisted of "two acts." The first act comprised his lifelong struggle against autocratic powers and oppressive forces against liberty. This period is thought to have consumed his early life and defined the first part of his papacy, until the collapse of the Soviet Union in 1991. The second act consisted of a sort of about-face, many believe, as he saw the need to restrain many aspects of the new kind of freedom he had a hand in bringing about. There is some truth to this, but to set these two "acts" in opposition to one another ultimately fails to understand the nuances of how Pope John Paul II defined human freedom throughout his life, including his entire papacy.

For Pope John Paul II, communism was only a single occasion brought about through the crisis of modernity that degraded the fundamental dignity and uniqueness of each and every human person. While communism, and Nazism before it, were blatant examples of this crisis, human beings could also experience dehumanization in free societies. John Stuart Mill is often deemed the father of "liberalism," who advanced a notion of human liberty based on a "utilitarian" philosophy that made "usefulness," rather than an innate dignity, the barometer of human value and virtue.

Accordingly, when the obvious violators of human dignity—the Nazis and communists—were no more, Pope John Paul II turned to what he thought had the potential to prove even more dangerous, mostly because its encroachment upon human dignity was less obvious. Whether against totalitarian regimes or in response to secular utilitarian ideologies, Pope John Paul II's papacy was united by a consistent defense of the biblical vision of the human person against false humanisms. What these false humanisms had in common was the error that human dignity began with humanity itself, with some kind of re-evaluation of a person's value based on what a person does, how much he or she contributes to society, or to what social class or political regime the person belongs.

# Theology of the Body

Near the end of 1979, John Paul II began what would eventually extend to 129 general audience addresses, spanning four years, which altogether formed what is arguably his most famous and enduring work: *Theology of the Body.* It is impossible to do justice to these lectures in such a small space. Thus, the reader is encouraged to peruse either a collection of the lectures or one of the many summaries of his work, especially Carl Anderson and Jose Granados' *Called to Love: Approaching John Paul II's Theology of the Body.* As the latter summarized it, for John Paul II, the experience of love is the foundation of what it means to be a human. Since this is the case, the human being cannot be reduced to a mere individual, for love necessitates relationships with others. Love removes us from all selfishness and confounds the narcissism of the modern era. It ushers us instead into a fullness of life that is revealed when the human being encounters others. Love transcends the individual; therefore, love connects the human being to the very transcendence of God, who, likewise out of love, created the world—not because He lacked anything in Himself, but because it was His very nature to love.

In short, during the course of his lectures, John Paul II began where Jesus Himself began when He was confronted with the question of divorce and remarriage (Matthew 19; Mark 10): He returned "to the beginning," in Genesis 1–3. Here John Paul II defines a number of "original experiences" that reveal the meaning and purpose of human existence. The first man begins to recognize what John Paul II terms his "original solitude"— that is, his uniqueness amongst all of God's creatures, when God parades before him all of the animals in a quest to identify a suitable helper (Genesis 2:19). As John Paul II put it in his *Roman Triptych,* man finds he is "alone in his wonderment, among many beings incapable of wonder." While this solitude does lead man to recognize that he is uniquely suited to love God, and to be loved by God, if this relationship is going to find expression in his earthly life, there still needs to be someone with whom man can participate in an exchange of love that mirrors God's love of man.

Accordingly, the first time God declares that something is "not good" in the Bible comes in recognition that it is not good for man to be alone (Genesis 2:20). Thus, God puts man into a "torpor," and from his very body, He fashions for the first man a wife. This is not merely a story about how Adam got a wife. It is, rather, a recognition that in spousal unity, humanity finally realizes its potential and purpose. This is why marriage itself—not simply the rite of matrimony—has a sacramental dimension for John Paul II. The "spousal meaning" of the body is a participation in the sort of love that God Himself offers and desires from all people. Marriage is an icon that depicts the mysteries of God's heart.

In describing how sin has impacted the human image, John Paul begins with a concept of "original nakedness" that shows how man exist in an unashamed state, gladly receiving the other's body as a gift and offering his own body to the other in return. This is contrasted with the "original shame" that follows after man and woman fall into sin. The issue with the original sin is not only that man disobeyed God but that man and woman ceased to live according to the rule of the gift. Rather than living in gratitude for what one is given, and offering oneself to the other in return, they seize a fruit that was not given to them, and this turns the gaze of man and woman away from a life defined by selflessness to one of exploitation. Man and woman experience "original shame" in their nakedness, then, because their lives are now consumed by exploitation rather than gift. Now, each sees the other as an object to use in satisfaction of one's own passions rather than joyfully receiving the other.

Again, it is virtually impossible to do justice to the rich significance of John Paul II's *Theology of the Body* in so little space. Suffice it to say, however, that these insights provided a new framework whereby Catholics (and even Protestants who found the pope's work on the topic insightful) a new language whereby they could engage a world that had been bent inward by the Sexual Revolution. For instance, unable to predict the plague that pornography would become in the twenty-first century on account of its proliferation on the Internet, John Paul II warned in one of his lectures that pornography does violence to the body not only by objectifying the "other" but also by objectifying oneself. When one indulges in pornography, one exploits another's body and does violence to that person by separating the person depicted from his or her body. This also does violence to one's own body: by uniting oneself to an "image" or a "body" stripped of its personhood, one subjects one's own body to exploitation and objectification. In other words, by indulging in pornography, a person cheats his or her own body from the deep, spousal love for which the human body was designed.

Secular views on homosexuality, likewise, miss the point. One does not possess a new "meaning" or "identity" simply because one's passions seek bodies of the same gender to exploit. To argue that we should be free to love "whomever we want" regardless of biological gender is to fail to understand the gift-giving dynamic that defines the spousal union of the body. When Adam awakes from his torpor and expresses his gratitude for woman, his joy is not derived from physical attraction to her. Rather, it is on account of the fact that she was made perfectly for him, and given him by God.

The problem in the post-Sexual Revolution world, it seems, in John Paul II's estimation—even in heterosexual relationships—is that people have come to believe that sexual attraction is the starting point of romantic love. Biblically speaking, physical attraction follows from embracing the gift-giving pattern of spousal love; it is not the basis for it. Accordingly, that one might be physically attracted to members of the same sex is no more justification for redefining marriage, in John Paul II's view, than the fact that a heterosexual finds women other than his wife physically attractive would justify polygamy or adultery. The point of marriage is not to satisfy our biological, sexual urges. It is, instead, to usher us into a relationship that exemplifies God's love in the world.

# Other Writings and Acts

Throughout Pope John Paul II's career, similar themes in his teaching reemerged in new contexts to address a myriad of social challenges and problems. In the encyclical *Laborem Exercens* (1981), John Paul II teaches that through work, men and women both participate in the Creator's original act that called everything into being. By working, we are called to "imitate God." Unlike the communists, who believe that work serves the state, John Paul II insists that our work is a way of putting us into contact with God. Work serves one's neighbor and, thus, is an expression of selfless love. John Paul II undoubtedly was articulating many of the conclusions he drew earlier in life when he was forced into hard labor under the Nazi regime.

In the apostolic letter *Salvifici Doloris* (1984), or *Redemptive Suffering*, Pope John Paul II teaches that while suffering in the world continues on account of sin, the suffering Christian is not without hope. Because Jesus entered into our suffering through the Cross, when we suffer, we find Jesus already there. We can identify our pain with Jesus' pain and therein find a deeper mystery of redemption, which is also the mystery of human liberation. Here, the language of "liberation" stood in contrast to liberation theologies and Marxist ideologies, which seek liberation through force and power. John Paul II insisted that liberation is discovered by the oppressed when, in their sufferings, they find Christ, who suffers alongside them and ushers them through their suffering into a life defined by resurrection and victory.

In John Paul II's 1985 apostolic letter, *The Youth of the World*, he contends that youth is an important time in life because it is in our youthful years that we begin to discover ourselves as moral actors. In one's youth, one begins to consider a personal future and a vocation in which one attempts to "read the eternal thought which god the Creator and Father has in their regard." Pope John Paul II knew how formative youthful years could be, as he attributed his endurance under persecuting regimes to the deep piety that had been nurtured in him first through his father and, subsequently, through various mentors. Thus, the pope emphasized that preparing the church's youth should be amongst its most important tasks. This is not only so that the next generation of the Church might discover leaders but also so that young people might be adequately prepared to encounter God personally, no matter what the future holds.

John Paul II's fourth encyclical, *Slavorum Apostoli* (1985), was written to address issues of "inculturation"—that is, how the gospel is best communicated to indigenous cultures in light of Vatican II. The letter emphasizes that no culture is more native to the gospel than any other and, thus, all cultures should be respected. Moreover, the human values upheld in any culture should be brought to a full light through the gospel. Thus, Pope John Paul II was open to unique expressions in the Church's liturgies in native cultures to the extent that they represented the universal human values of the culture.

His 1986 encyclical, *Dominum et Vivificantem,* is a treatise on the Holy Spirit. Here, Pope John Paul II emphasizes that the Holy Spirit is the person of the Trinity through whom we experience God's "being with" the world. It is the Holy Spirit who takes what Jesus accomplished in history and makes the cross and resurrection a present reality in our daily lives. It is the Holy Spirit who draws us into a direct encounter with God, introducing us to the Son, who mediates our relationship with the Father. The Holy Spirit illumines our conscience so that we can call evil, evil, and good, good. This particular encyclical was also widely embraced by Eastern Christianity. When, shortly after its publication, a delegation from the Ecumenical Patriarchate of Constantinople came to meet John Paul II in Rome, it marked an initial step on a journey (which is still underway) that might eventually lead to reconciliation between Orthodoxy and Catholicism.

In 1988 John Paul II penned *Mulieris Dignitatem* on the dignity and vocation of women. It represented his most concerted effort to counter the claim of some feminists that Christianity is inherently misogynist. "In God's eternal plan," he wrote, "woman is the one in whom the order of love in the created world of persons first takes root." In women, the order of love connects us to God's order of justice and charity, which is integral to understanding the human experience and the dignity of persons. In Genesis, it was not good that man should be alone. The same holds true in the present. Man and woman, therefore, are equally dignified before God.

That does not mean, however, that man and woman are *identical*. Woman is not honored when what should be celebrated about woman uniquely is discounted and she tries to be more like a man. Neither is a man dignified when he is ashamed by his masculinity and tries to be more feminine. Both man and woman are equally dignified before God, which means the equality of men and women is upheld when we embrace the masculine and feminine as equal and necessary components of God's design for humanity.

His eighth encyclical, *Redemptoris Missio, The Mission of the Redeemer*, emphasizes that the Church does not merely have a mission—the Church *is* a mission. Here John Paul II rejects the post-Vatican II notion that the Church's mission to the nations has been completed. He also rejects the idea that the Church's mission was a form of imperialism, imposing Christianity on an "unenlightened" world that neither wants nor needs it. The mission, he argues, is not a footnote to the Church's doctrine concerning the Church. The Church is a mission precisely because God's mission is located in the doctrine of God as Trinity and in the doctrine of Jesus' Incarnation.

The Trinity, in self-giving, forms the pattern for the Church's community of self-giving missionaries. The Incarnation demonstrates that God actively seeks us—we do not primarily seek God and define Him however we like. He comes to us, making no apologies for Himself or His teaching, and saves us even when we misunderstand His intentions. While other religions might reflect certain eternal truths, apart from Jesus Christ they do not offer true salvation. If anyone is to be saved, he or she must be saved through Jesus Christ. This is not a message of exclusion, as some claim, but a message of inclusion. Jesus came into the world so that all the world might be saved. That some refuse this invitation is not His fault. Someone dangling from a cliff does not complain when someone offers a hand because the person in jeopardy had hoped to be saved in another way. Instead, in one's peril, one grips the hand that is offered and gives up on the notion that we can design our own path toward salvation.

# Aging Gracefully

An assassination attempt was made on Pope John Paul II's life in 1981. Agca, a professional assassin, fired at the pope at point-blank range, but the bullet missed his main abdominal artery by a fraction of an inch. It also missed his spinal column. The pope recovered in a miraculously short amount of time. While it remains debated what Agca's motivation was, many believed the attempt was directed by the Soviet KGB. Regardless, the Italian court initially sentenced Agca to life in prison.

Immediately after the shooting, however, Pope John Paul II exhorted the people to "pray for my brother … who I have sincerely forgiven." In 1983, Pope John Paul II met his would-be assassin in prison. Agca was seen kissing his ring at the end of their meeting, and while he had earlier said that he felt the pope had been "the incarnation of all that is capitalism," he called the pope a friend later in life. Indeed, the pope intervened and asked the Italian government to grant him a pardon. They followed his wishes, and Agca was extradited to Turkey. When Pope John Paul II died, reports suggested that Agca deeply mourned the Holy Father's death.

The episode exemplifies a degree of Christ-like piety, modeled after Jesus' own exhortation to the Father that He forgive Jesus' executioners, who knew not what they were doing. Such mercy confounded the world's sense of justice. For John Paul II, God's sense of justice is derived from His character of love steeped in forgiveness, which demands a justice founded in mercy rather than revenge. Reconciliation, therefore, was a driving force in John Paul II's piety. In 1998, in fact, he signed the test of the Joint Declaration on the Doctrine of Justification, which marked a first-step in healing the divide between Catholicism and Lutheranism that had persisted since the sixteenth century.

John Paul II was diagnosed with Parkinson's disease in 1994. Initially, this made it more difficult for him to walk and caused a tremor in his left arm and hand. For the next decade, the world saw his condition worsen, but his spirit never faded. He continued to produce encyclicals defending human rights and the truth of God's word. He continued to visit all parts of the globe, and even though it caused him great physical pain, he appeared regularly before crowds. Unlike many who struggle with physical challenges in their old age, however, he graciously accepted the help of his aides. He recognized that by allowing them to help him, he was giving them the opportunity to participate in the servanthood of Christ. To insist on trying to do everything himself would deprive them of such an opportunity.

To age gracefully is to age with a life full of grace. This is precisely the way that Pope John Paul II lived out his final years. Even as his body began to fail, and the tremors of Parkinson's made it almost painful to watch his decline, his mind remained sharp. His voice, shaky though it had become in tone, remained unwavering in its content. John Paul II aged with grace as he received the gifts of others and offered himself to the world in return.

# Chapter Eight: Sainted and Remembered

John Paul II died on April 2, 2005, at eighty-four years of age. Not long after his death, many clergy at the Vatican and people throughout the world began referring to him as John Paul the Great. He was only the fourth pope ever to receive this recognition, and the first since the first millennium. While no formal process establishes this title in canon law, custom dictates the honorarium.

During John Paul II's funeral mass, the chant *"Santo Subito!"* erupted. It means "Make him a Saint now!" Pope Benedict XVI began the beatification process and authorized bypassing the usual five-year waiting period that is required after one's death before the process can begin. Reportedly, a French nun who had been diagnosed with Parkinson's disease was immediately cured after praying and asking John Paul II to intercede on her behalf. Pope Benedict XVI confirmed the miracle on January 14, 2011. He was officially beatified as Pope St. John Paul II on May 1, 2011, at the Feast of Divine Mercy. Additional miracles have since been attributed to those who have asked Pope St. John Paul II to intercede for them, one of which was confirmed by Pope Francis on July 4, 2013. The canonization mass was celebrated on April 27, 2014, by both Pope Francis and Pope Emeritus Benedict XVI. More than 500,000 people attended his mass, an assembly only rivaled by the historic crowd that had heard his liberating words in Warsaw in 1979.

Few lives have been so steeped in a Christ-defined love, and few lives have inspired so many others to follow Christ's path in love, as that of Karol Wojtyla, who became Pope St. John Paul II. In a world that valued people based on their utility, John Paul II proclaimed that every human being has an inherent dignity and is valuable. In a therapeutic era that decried pain and advocated for assuaging it by any means possible, John Paul II upheld the biblical truth that suffering can be redemptive and that true happiness comes by living according to God's design rather than by pursuing human passions.

Pope St. John Paul II was a modern man who upheld an ancient truth and found no conflict between the two. He was a staunch defender of human liberty, but it was a liberty defined by the dignity that God ascribed to humanity as testified in Scripture. He was a brave confessor under the thumb of two oppressive regimes and inspired a nation—and eventually the world—to stand firm in their faith no matter what hardships they might face. He believed that oppression must be resisted, but not through force. Oppressors and tyrants are conquered not through the strength of arms, but through love.

This means more than pursuing the path of love in the midst of political tyrants. The love of Christ should define our personal lives. When he forgave his own would-be assassin, and even petitioned for his pardon, Pope St. John Paul II testified to the power of God's love in transforming wayward lives and redeeming even murderers and the worst of sinners in mercy.

Printed in Great Britain
by Amazon